(

I THOUGHT I WAS A CHRISTIAN, BUT I WENT TO HELL

CONVERTED

I THOUGHT I WAS A CHRISTIAN, BUT I WENT TO HELL

By Barry J. Holcomb

Published by
MIDNIGHT EXPRESS BOOKS

CONVERTED

I THOUGHT I WAS A CHRISTIAN, BUT I WENT TO HELL

ISBN-13 978-0-9903183-1-6
ISBN-10 0990318311

Published by
MIDNIGHT EXPRESS BOOKS
POBox 69
Berryville AR 72616
(870) 210-3772
MEBooks1@yahoo.com

CONVERTED

I THOUGHT I WAS A CHRISTIAN, BUT I WENT TO HELL

By Barry J. Holcomb

SPECIAL THANKS

This book is dedicated to my Lord and Savior Jesus Christ. Thank you Lord for giving me an undeserved second chance at life and salvation. Thank you Mom for always being there for me no matter how bad I messed up. To my beautiful daughter Brittnie. I know we have never had a traditional father, daughter relationship, yet we have made the best of what we have. I am incredibly proud of you. It has given me great pleasure watching you grow into a young woman. You will always be daddy's little girl. Cody, I love you son and pray God will keep you and bless you.

INTRODUCTION

This book tells the story of a man who lived his life trying to fill the void in his heart with the things of the world. Drugs, women, and money were the only things he was concerned with. This led him into a life of crime.

His life of crime came to an abrupt halt one night when in a drunken pill-induced stupor he took the life of the woman he loved and their unborn son. He was sentenced to spend the rest of his life in prison for his crime.

In prison, his drug use got worse and worse until the night he went too far and died from a heroin overdose.

Barry had spent his life ‘believing’ the story he heard about Jesus and he thought he was a Christian. The night he died he stood at the gates of hell waiting to enter and found out he had been fooling himself. Not only was he not a Christian, but he was on his way to hell. A second chance at life compelled Barry to dedicate his life to Jesus.

Now he is sure he is a Christian and he lives every day of his life in grateful service to the Lord that has filled the void in his heart and shown him undeserved mercy.

Contents

PART ONE

CHAPTER 1 – The Beginning

Hello, my name is Barry Holcomb. I came into this world on October 29th, 1972. My parents were married after my mom got pregnant with me, and they were divorced before I was out of diapers. The old saying about it taking a village to raise a kid was true in my case. My mom was only 17 when she had me so she needed help taking care of me. My mom is the youngest of four, with three older brothers. Thanks to her brothers and her mom, we survived my toddler years. My mom is a strong woman and did what it took to take care of me the best she could. My dad had gone his own way after the divorce. With the exception of a few occasions I was not around him until I was in my teens. My mom used to let me go to his parent's house and they would watch me from time to time. They would take me to church on Sundays, while I was at their house. That was when I was first introduced to Jesus.

When I was three my mom got remarried to a man who called himself "Bubba". He did not think I needed to go around my dad's family any more. So my trips to Grandma and Grandpa Holcomb's pretty much came to an end.

I still went down there every once in a while. My mom made sure I went down there for Easter so they could take me to church if she did not take me. Easter and funerals were the only times my mom went to church. Although my mom and Bubba both believed in God, God was not a part of our everyday lives on any level.

My dad refused to pay any child-support or have anything to do with me, so Bubba figured I would be better off without any of the Holcomb's in my life. He decided he was going to be my dad. I don't remember when it happened, but I started calling him dad.

Bubba was from southern Louisiana. He was of the school of thought that children were to be seen and not heard. He also believed his belt was the answer for every mistake I made. It seemed like he found a reason to whip me with that belt three of four times a week. I never will forget the sound his belt buckle made when he took it off. His belt was made of thick leather, and the buckle had two prongs on it that rang like a bell as he walked down the hall toward my room. What started out as fear quickly became hatred for both that belt, and him. I am a believer in spanking a child, but the consequences for over doing it can be very great. The sad thing is, I believe he like most people who abuse their kids, actually thought what he was doing was right. As I said earlier, my mom was young when she had me. So she really did not know any better herself, and her dad had punished her brothers the same way. Although I do not blame the treatment I received as a child for how I turned out, I do blame it for teaching me how to hate, and not fear consequences for my actions. After a while I became calloused to getting whipped, and I did not care about consequences for doing wrong.

Growing up, I was the kid who was always the first to try something. If someone built a ramp, I tested it out. I was the first kid on my block to smoke a cigarette. It usually did not take long for the neighbors to figure out I was not the best kid for their kid to hang out with. By the time I was 8 or 9, I became immune to the belt. I lost all fear of it and what it represented. I figured I was going to get it at least a couple times a week anyway, so I might as well do as I pleased. Don't get me wrong I was not blatantly disrespectful and I did everything possible to get away with my antics. It did not take me long to figure out I could be the cool kid if I took everything a step further than the next kid was willing to go.

On top of being an extreme disciplinarian, Bubba was an alcoholic and marijuana addict. When he and my mom first got married he had a good job and worked regularly. His drinking and pot smoking led to him losing a couple of good jobs. Sometimes he would not work for months at a time. I think the longest he went without working was two years. This caused us to have to move around all the time. People are kind of funny about not wanting you to live in their houses if you don't pay the rent. A few times we would have to live with family or friends. Bubba's alcohol problem caused my mom and him to fight more than they got along. Many times their battles turned physical and on more than one occasion I found myself in the middle of it. They would split up for awhile then get back together again. While they were separated I would usually go stay with one of my uncles or my mom's dad,

Grandpa A.J. This was an ongoing pattern until they finally split up when I was thirteen. I never could figure out why none of my mom's brothers would come rescue us. I guess they figured she was a big girl and could take care of herself.

After they split up my mom thought it would be a good idea for me to get re-acquainted my dad's family. My dad's brother Gary, (my mom and dad both have brothers named Gary) would let me come and spend weekends with him and his wife. I think my dad was in Texas at that time. I was told he went there to avoid paying child-support. My Uncle Gary had nice cars and the best clothes and shoes on the market. His pockets were always full of money. He had more friends than I could count. There was always people coming in and out of his house and they all seemed to look up to Gary. It did not take me long to figure out Uncle Gary was a drug dealer. It wasn't long before he was letting me smoke pot with him and his friends. He thought it was funny to get me stoned, and I thought it made me cool. He became someone I wanted to be like. My mom and all her brothers worked hard for their money. Working no longer seemed like a good idea. I finally knew what I wanted to be when I grew up. I wanted to be a drug dealer.

CHAPTER 2 – The Go-Cart

My mom did not have any idea what went on during my weekend trips to Uncle Gary's. She never had any reason to think he would give me drugs, so she continued to let me go to his house pretty much every weekend, and for longer periods during the summer. Mom had moved us to the suburbs to get me into better schools. It did not matter what school she put me in, I always found a way to get myself kicked out. I was a smart kid and had no problem doing school work. My problem was I liked drinking and getting high and running with a group of kids who did not care about school either. I quickly became the cool kid in the neighborhood, because I could score weed for us any time we came up with the money for it. Before long I was making numerous trips to my uncle's house in the city every week.

Along with getting high, this was about the time I became a thief. Me and the group of guys I ran around with would steal anything that was not bolted down. We were not picky. Sometimes we would go out at night and break into cars. We would steal anything that had a motor. I could not count the number of dirt bikes and four-wheelers we took from people. Looking back it is hard to believe how little regard we had for other people's property.

All the stealing led to my first run in with the law when I was fourteen. A neighbor of ours had a go-cart in their garage. I had approached them to see if they would sell it to me. I had money, and my plan was to actually buy it from them. They said "no," they did not want to sell it. Well, I had done set my mind on getting that go-cart, and the way I saw it was, they were like eighty years old and did not need a go-cart. One night a few weeks later me and a buddy were on our way home from the Square. That was where us kids liked to hang out and smoke pot and drink on the weekends. I was pretty lit up, and I told him we should go get the go-cart. He told me he was going home but for me to go check and see if the garage door was open. If it was, he wanted me to come back and get him and we would steal the go-cart. When I got there, the garage door was not locked. Rather than going to get my buddy I went on in the garage and took the go-cart.

Showing up at home with a go-cart was not hard to explain to my mom.

I was always working on one of the neighbor kid's bikes or dirt bike, so my mom did not suspect anything when I told her me and my buddy built the go-cart. I was always very mechanically inclined. I could take apart almost anything that had a motor, put it back together, and it would run right more times than not. I took that go-cart apart and fixed a few things that were wrong with the brakes. I gave it a new paint job so no one would recognize it.

Well, you can imagine the surprise my mom got when the police knocked on her front door. They ask her if there was a go-cart on the property. She told them just the one her son and his friend had built. They asked if they could see it so she raised the garage door and showed them "my" go cart. Needless to say mom was not very happy to find out it was not a home-made go-cart but a very expensive store-bought go-cart that had been stolen out of an old couple's garage.

Lucky for me, I was at school when the go-cart was found. I knew something was wrong when I was told not to ride the bus home; my cousin would be there to pick me up. When I got in the car he would not tell me what was going on. As soon as we pulled in the driveway I looked in the garage and to my utter horror the go-cart was gone. At the time it hadn't dawned on me that a go-cart stolen from a block and a half away could be traced back to me. It turned out the lady who lived across the street from us had called the police and complained about me and my friends riding dirt-bikes and go-carts up and down the street all day. The police told my mom to bring me to the police station the next day, and to bring the friend who had helped me build the go-cart.

My mom was so mad she did not know what to do with herself, so she hit on me for a while. My mom is a little woman so it really didn't hurt, but I understood she was mad. You see, not only had I lied about where the go-cart came from, I had let her and her new boyfriend drive it. One night they were in the driveway talking when I came home on it. Reno (her boyfriend) seemed pretty interested in it, so I asked him if he wanted to drive it. Then my mom took a turn. They had the time of their lives driving my stolen go-cart up and down the street. That day the police told Mom the go-cart was stolen, she made sure the top of my head knew how much she appreciated my generosity in letting her drive a stolen go-cart. I remember the whole time they were driving it I was praying a cop did not come down the street.

I had no choice but to go in and confess to stealing the go-cart. The people remembered me coming to them and asking about buying it, but they chose not to pursue charges. They got their go-cart back with a new paint job, and it ran better than it did when I took it.

The police, however, were not so willing to let me off the hook. The detective I talked to put me on a 90-day probation. He said if I stayed out of trouble he would see to it the go-cart theft did not go on my record. I was more than happy to agree with him. I walked down the probation without a problem. After that I was much more careful about the crimes I committed. I no longer kept any of the things I stole. I would use it then leave it when I was done. There are numerous dirt bikes, four-wheelers, and even a dune buggy back on the trails where we rode.

It was brought to my attention that a person could order white crosses from a place that advertised on the back of porno-magazines. These were really just ephedrine pills, but the kids at school never knew the difference. The company would let you order 1,000 pills for $15.00. I turned around and sold them for 50¢ apiece. This was a lot of money for a fourteen year old. I always managed to spend it. Up to that point my mom thought I was making money on my paper route, and fixing bikes and stuff. If I ever needed a little extra cover, my Uncle Gary would say he gave me the money. I was amazed at how easy it was to spend a bunch of money and have absolutely nothing to show for it.

All of this took place around the time my mom started dating Reno. Her life was pretty much consumed with the new relationship. My grandma was living with us at that time. She made sure I did not catch the house on fire again. Yeah, when I was 8, I was smoking in the little storage room in our basement. I caught the tassels of a rug on fire and the fire spread quickly from there. No one got hurt, except me after the firemen left. Grandma was my buddy.

She would cover for me all the time when I did stupid

stuff. One time I thought it would be funny to taze her. Well, she did not think it was as funny as I did and she broke a broom over my head. She laughed about it....a few years later. Anyway, Reno was a good man. He had a regular job and had his life together. He never attempted to be a dad, but always tried to be my friend. I gave him the blues most of the time, but honestly I looked up to him and respected him greatly, and I still do till this day. He and my mom got a real nice house and we all moved in together. This was the nicest house I had ever been in. It even had an in-ground pool with a diving board in our back yard. This was my proverbial fork in the road. This was my chance to get myself together and get on the right path, do good in school and make something of myself. My mom and Reno would have supported me all the way. Regretfully, by this time I had already made up my mind I wanted to be a career criminal.

Before I turned 16, the school finally had enough of me. They told my mom to take me home and not to send me back any more. They had tried everything to get me to act right. They even sent me to a school for boys. I guess they thought girls were my problem. Which at that time they were more than a distraction. The boy's school did not work out either, so my time in the public school system came to an end. At that time this was fine with me, I had no need for the stuff they were teaching anyway. Now I had more time to do the things I enjoyed, getting high and running wild.

It was not long before I had my next run-in with the law. The only problem with not going to school is I had a lot of extra time on my hands. Even though we were living in a much nicer neighborhood, it did not take me long to find some like-minded kids who liked drinking and getting high.

One of the neighbor boys and I were out getting high and he told me about how the guy that lived on the corner left the keys in his car. We decided we would meet up later that night and 'borrow' his car for a little while.

Imagine that man's surprise when the town police called him and asked if he had let us use his car. Needless to say, off to jail we went. I thought my mom was going to kill me when she got there to pick me up. For the first time in my life I actually felt shame for something I did wrong. She was fulfilling all her dreams of having a nice man, and a nice house in a good neighborhood, and I had embarrassed her to the point of humiliation. I loved my mom more than life itself and it bothered me that I had hurt her so bad that day.

They gave me a court date at the Juvenile Justice Center. My mom was at her wit's end with me. She had tried everything to get me to act right, but nothing worked, so she put me in a mental hospital that specialized in figuring out what was wrong with kids. They sent me home 45 days later, just as broken as I was when I got there.

CHAPTER 3 - California

I had about two months until my court date when I was released from the mental hospital. I went to work for a family friend power-washing semi trucks. All I did for those two months was work and spend time with my girlfriend. My paychecks went straight to my mom so I could pay for a lawyer. When the kid that was with me went to court the judge lifted the restriction on his driver's license and sent him home. He had been caught driving before he had his license a couple times, so they had suspended his license until he was 18. After seeing what happened to him, I knew I was going to get off easy. Even though he was the one driving the car when we were pulled over, he told them it was all my fault and he was just an innocent kid that got caught running with the wrong person. I was not aware of what all he had told the police until the day I was sitting in the court room. The judge did not give me a chance to say anything; he sentenced me to 45 days in a juvenile halfway house. I was sent home to wait on a bed to open so I could go start my time. I know 45 days does not sound like a long time, but to a 15 year old it might as well have been 45 years.

When the day came for me to go start my time I told my girlfriend bye, then headed off to serve my sentence. When I first arrived at Nate Lynn halfway house it seemed okay. All we did was sit around and do nothing with our time. I spent most of my time sneaking off to smoke. It was against the rules, but most of the staff didn't care as long as you did not do it in their face. There was one staff member who disliked me for some reason. I had not done anything to her; she just did not like me. One day another kid and I were upstairs smoking and one of the other kids went and told on us. The staff woman who disliked me went outside and looked up at the window I was leaning out, she busted me. Most of the time when you were caught breaking a rule they would make you clean up the house by yourself. She decided she was going to take my weekend home pass. I thought that was a little extreme. It just so happened my 16th birthday fell on that weekend, and I already had plans. That Friday night I called my cousin and told him to meet me out front, I was going to escape that night. Around midnight I tossed a bag of clothes out the second story window and I followed them. In hindsight, I could have just walked out the front door, they never locked it. Jumping out the window made it feel more like an escape though.

We ran a few blocks to the 7-11 store and I called a taxi. My cousin went to his house and I went to my Uncle Gary's house. He paid for the cab and I settled in for the night. A few hours later my mom was at the door. I could not figure out how she found me so fast until I saw my cousin sitting there in the front seat of the car. She took me back to the halfway house. They had a rule if you returned within 24 hours they would not kick you out. When I got back the other kids had a good laugh at my expense. That was okay; at least I got to smoke a little weed for my birthday.

What I did not know was when they asked my mom why she thought I had left; she told them I was afraid the other kids were going to beat me up. There were 14 of us in the house and I was the only white kid. I never had any trouble with any of the kids. We all got along pretty good. The staff lady, who did not like me, thought it was a good idea to announce in front of everyone that I ran off because the black kids were going to beat me up. We were all sitting in the T.V. room when this took place. I remember sitting there in shock. I had no idea where she came up with that. Of course I denied it, but there was no way to convince those 13 black kids the white kid had not used them as an excuse for running off.

Now I did have a reason to worry. I could tell by the look in their eyes something bad was about to happen. That night I stole a pair of scissors out of the craft box, and I busted a bottle in half. I took my weapons to bed with me. One of the kids who I had known since the 4th grade came into my room the next morning and told me I better get out of there. It seems the other kids had got themselves all worked up into a rage to beat me up. I told him I would fight them one at a time if they wanted to, but they all wanted to jump me at once. I could fight a little bit and I was always up to a good challenge, but this did not seem like a good idea at all. So once again, I went out the second story window. This time I did not tell anyone where I was going.

I am pretty sure my mom knew I went to Gary's house again. Only this time when she showed up he told her he had not seen me. I stayed on the run for about a month. I stayed with my aunt Betty Holcomb. She fixed me up with her boyfriend's sister, Becky. She became my first serious girlfriend. I had been with a few girls before her. My sex life started when I was 12, but she was different. I loved her, and she loved me. She was just as wild as me and she loved having a bad boy for a boyfriend.

After a while my aunt got tired of me sleeping on her couch and I could not go to Gary's because the police were watching the house. My grandma Holcomb got word to me that I needed to call my mom.

I went to a pay phone and called her. She was relieved to hear from me, and it was nice to hear her voice as well. She told me she wanted me to come home. I told her turning myself in was not an option. She said I could go live with my uncle Darrell in California. I made her swear she was not setting me up. She told me to come home and I would be on a plane the next morning. She wanted me out of the city before something bad happened.. I guess she figured if I was going to run I might as well be where she knew I would be safe.

The next morning I was on my way to California to stay with my uncle and his wife. At that time he was a big shot at a company that supplied work uniforms to businesses. I went to work for him for a while cleaning up the shop and office areas. Then I found a job at a gas station. I bought a 10-speed bicycle for transportation. I knew the best way to get caught by the police was in a car. My job was pretty easy. I started out pumping gas in the full service section. Then I was promoted to working the cash register from 10:00 p.m. till 5:00 a.m. Becky and I talked on the phone pretty much every day. The plan was for me to save up enough money for her to come out there and live with me.

I met some new friends who liked to get high and could supply me with some weed. These friends introduced me to crystal meth. Up to that point in my life I had only drank, smoked pot and ate a few pills. Meth was a whole new world. It was not long before Becky was mad at me and decided she was not coming out there. She told me if I wanted to be with her I was going to have to come home. I was stealing money out of my cash register to pay for the dope I was doing. I had a clever way of skimming money. I figured I would not get caught until they did inventory. Before that happened, I decided I was going back to Kansas City. I waited until Friday night to make my move. I did not make a cash drop all night.

I had taken in almost $800.00 that night. I put the cash in an envelope and wrapped it up with duct tape. I hid the money outside by the dumpsters.

Then I went back in and called the police and told them I had been robbed.

They came to the gas station and made their report and then sent me home.

I doubled back and collected the money and went back to my uncle's apartment. My plan was to wait for him and his wife to leave for work then I was going to head for the airport. I had not been to sleep for three days and when I lay down in the bed I passed out. The next thing I knew it was 8:00 p.m. and the police were beating on the front door. They made it to the bedroom before I could make it out the window. It was probably good they did, because we were three stories up and I would have been jumping onto concrete. It was never made clear exactly how they found out I had a missing person warrant in Missouri.

They took me to a Juvenile facility to await extradition

back to Missouri. When I got to the facility they put me in a room by myself for a week. They did this to all new guys to see how you were going to act. I never will forget that room. They pumped some of the most awful music imaginable into my room through a speaker in the ceiling. I am pretty sure the only two songs that played were, Tone Lokes "Funky Cole Madena" and Bobby Brown's "That's My Prerogative." That little speaker quickly became my archenemy. My time in that cell was the first time I read the Bible. It was the only book I could get my hands on. That was the first time I ask God to save me. I had gone forward in church when I was little, but I did not know what I was doing. During my time in that cell I ask God to fix me. I knew I was broken and the lifestyle I was living was not helping me at all. There had always been a vacant spot in my heart that I tried to fill with every form of debauchery possible, but nothing filled that void. For the first time in my life I no longer felt the void in my heart. I wish I could have stayed in that room a little longer.

Just when I was finding peace within myself they came and moved me to a pod which held about 75 kids. Within an hour of being in there I had forgotten everything I had found in the Bible. This place was tough. The first thing I had to do was fight to get my mattress back from a kid who thought he needed two mattresses. I knew right away this place was not going to be any fun. I spent the next three weeks watching my back. Being from Missouri I was an outsider, thus the enemy. I only had to fight a couple times but the tension in that place was so thick you could cut it with a knife. It was a very happy day when they took me to court and ask me if I would sign extradition papers. I asked the guy there what would happen if I refused to sign then. He told me I would stay there for up to 6 months waiting on a Governor's Warrant from Missouri, but if I signed them I would be on a plane back to Kansas City that day. I snatched the pen out of his hand so fast it startled him. A couple hours later I was on a plane by myself headed home.

My plan was to take off the second the plane landed. To my surprise the Juvenile officer who had my case was waiting at the door of the airplane for me. He took me straight to the Juvenile Justice Center in Kansas City. After about 30 days they called me to dress out. This meant you were going home. I was quite surprised, but got dressed as fast as I could before they figured out their mistake. It was not a mistake; my mom and Reno were outside waiting on me. We had to go down town to a meeting with some juvenile officers. The meeting was in a big building. The room we went into was on the top floor. As soon as we went into the room a guy locked the doors with a key. It was at that point I realized I was not home free yet.

They informed me we were there to put together a home plan. My mom and them were going to tell me what they expected of me. If I disagreed with them I would go back to jail. If we came to an understanding I would go home. This was a no-brainer, I agreed with everything they said and went home. At that point I actually planned on getting a job and acting right. I went to work at a fast food restaurant. It was there I met Kim, my next true love. Sadly it was not long until that empty place in my heart started calling to be filled. Rather than submitting to God, I once again set out to fill it with the ways of the world.

CHAPTER 4 – My New Profession

The main stipulation to me going home was I could not go around my Uncle Gary any more. I think I held up that end of the agreement for about two weeks. As soon as I started smoking weed again I was back at his house on a regular basis. I was still trying to act right. I worked a few different jobs and was coming home at a decent hour every night. A couple months later I was released from all state supervision. After that, I went wild. Within about a week I moved out of my mom's house. Before long I was living with Gary in Kansas City. I made a little money working for him. Basically being a stooge, carrying dope from one place to another. This did not last very long. In fact it lasted just long enough for me to find out where most of the drug dealers in the Kansas City area lived. I also knew approximately how much product they were selling. I was formulating a new plan on how I was going to make a living.

One night my uncle's drug connection came to the house to collect some money. He had a duffel-bag full of money with him. There had to have been at least $200,000.00 in that bag. At one point his body guard went to the store next door, and he went to the bathroom. I asked my uncle why we did not just take the money from the guy; after all, he was not from the neighborhood? Gary said we could not do that because he made too much money through the guy. Later he told me if I thought I had the heart to rob people he would hook me up with some guys he knew. These guys turned out to be two brothers from the neighborhood. They were very dangerous men. My relationship with these two would change my life forever. They were in their 30's and both had already done time in prison. They made their money robbing drug dealers.

I would later find out they went to school with my mom. I thought she was going to have a nervous breakdown when she found out who my new friends were.

These guys were considered real gangsters, and people feared and respected them. I knew I was going to have to impress them or find myself in a real bad place real fast. The first robbery I did with them was a guy my uncle set up. This was a test for me. They sent me to the door by myself. My Job was to get in the house and get things under control then they would come in behind me. I put on a good front like I was eager to do it. In reality, I was so nervous I almost peed in my pants. Everything went smoothly, and after we made it out of the house with all the guy's drugs and money I knew I had found my new profession.

In the beginning all we robbed was drug dealers. As we earned more money we met more powerful people. It does not take long to climb the ladder in the criminal world. It did not dawn on me it was so easy to climb the ladder because so many people were falling off the ladder, making room for the next dummy. Before long the three of us had a reputation of getting the job done. We were smart, and made it a point not to hurt anyone. Before every job I would pray that none of the people we were robbing would get hurt. God answered this prayer and none of our victims got seriously hurt. Some jobs took a great deal of planning. As I said the number one goal was to figure out how to get in and out without having to hurt anyone. The brothers taught me early on that when you hurt people they might have to go to the hospital, and that brought the police into things. Not many drug dealers will call the police and tell them someone just took their dope. If they have to go to the hospital they would have to explain what happened to them. When people suffer trauma they tend to be very talkative. Plus if you hurt someone their loved ones would be a little more apt to retaliate against us. Keep in mind some of the people we were robbing knew who we were.

Before long we got hooked up with a guy who knew people that kept a lot of cash and jewels in their homes. His family owned businesses that would buy all the jewelry we brought them. After a while we added two more guys to our crew and we started taking down jewelry stores.

I started noticing something very strange, it did not matter how much money I made, I never got to keep any of it. By the time I was 19 I had gotten 9 D.W.I.s, those cost a minimum of $5,000.00 each. Often I would find my pockets empty and could not figure out how they got that way. My grandpa A.J. told me when I was a little boy, “You will never keep anything you get by doing wrong." I can't tell you how many times those words ran through my mind.

Then in the winter of 1989 I got my first felony conviction. Kim and I were on our way to pick up a friend of mine to go out and party. I had been eating Valium all day, I think I had eaten five or six by that time, and I had been drinking a few beers. I was very high. On my way into my buddy's apartment complex, I got into an argument with a car load of guys. I don't remember what started it, or how it escalated so fast. They jumped out of their car with tire tools and bats, and I jumped out of my car with a 20 gauge shotgun. That night God was in that parking lot with them and me, and He worked a miracle. I had the shotgun loaded with slugs and buck-shot. I pumped a shell into the chamber and pulled the trigger. Nothing happened.

I quickly pumped in another round; made sure the safety was off and squeezed the trigger again. Still nothing. Needless to say by this time they all took off running on foot. I panicked and took off myself. I ran and hid in the bushes behind one of the buildings. After a while I got the bright idea to go back and get my car. In case you are wondering what happened to Kim, I had forgot all about her, until I rounded the corner and saw about 100 cops around my car, with Kim standing there in hand-cuffs. I felt I needed to rescue her so I walked up to the cops and asked them what was going on. They drew their guns on me so fast I thought I was in the Wild West. They took me to jail and charged me with exhibiting a deadly weapon. I spent the night in jail and was released on bond the next morning. By this time I had a bondsman who was willing to post my bond anytime I went to jail.

Kim's mom had listened to the whole incident take place over her police scanner. Her mom knew my uncle and was not too happy about Kim going out with me. After that night Kim's mom's dislike for me turned to pure hatred. She forbade Kim from seeing me anymore. We continued to see each other for awhile. I greatly reduced Kim's exposure to my lifestyle. It did not take long before she got tired of not being able to be with me all the time. She thought every time we were apart I was messing with another woman, and sadly she was right most of the time. At that point in my life I felt it was best if I did not have a steady girl. I was on a path of self-destruction, and I did not want to take anyone else with me.

I hired a good lawyer to represent me on the gun case.

He got me sentenced to two years probation. This did not slow me down at all. If anything it made me feel more like a real criminal. My mind was so messed up, I thought bad was good, and good was bad. Drugs, power and money had made me crazy in the head.

After a time of bouncing from one girl to the next, I settled down with Jennifer. She knew what I did for a living. Unlike most of the girls I had been with, she did not nag at me to quit. It was a very odd relationship.

We were complete opposites. She was a good girl who did not do drugs or anything. She drank a little on the weekend, but nothing else. We got along great. She got pregnant and we were told we were going to have a little girl.

By this time the crew of guys I was working with had gone our separate ways. While I drank, smoked pot and ate pills from time to time, they were all addicted to shooting cocaine into their veins. They were able to control their addictions for a while, but towards the end they were completely out of control. They started doing high-risk/low-reward robberies. They wanted me to be the front man on a jewelry store robbery. After looking it over I decided nothing looked or felt right about this place. I told them I was not going to do it. One of the other guys took my place. The jewelry store owner gunned him down. That day a man I liked more than any of the others lost his life. I felt like the two brothers were responsible for his death. I never did another robbery with them. Their drug use had made them unreliable and unsafe to work with. I did a few things on my own after that, but the thrill of doing robberies was gone. I knew I had lost my edge and it was time to find a new profession.

I had almost finished walking down my probation. My plan was to get a job, settle down and have a family. Then this guy I knew called and wanted to buy a large quantity of pot. I did not like the guy so, I decided it would be okay to take his money. This was going to be my last score. It was going to give me enough money to have a head start at our new life. Come to find out, the guy did not like me very much either. He was setting me up with the police. I had planned it to where I would go in an apartment building to buy the pot and when I came out a buddy of mine pretended to rob me and take off with the pot. Everything went just as planned. It all happened so fast the cops who were watching everything did not realize what happened. They knew something had gone wrong, they just did not know what. At that time I still did not know the guy who was in the car with the guy I was ripping off was a cop. When I ran up to the car and told them I just got robbed the cop jumped out of the car telling me I better get his money. Before long the argument got physical and I felt his gun while we were wrestling over the hood of the car. At that point something in my head told me the guy was a cop. A drug dealer would have pulled the gun before he tried to fight with his hands. He definitely would have pulled it the moment he started losing the fight. Before I knew it here came another guy out of the dark. This guy claimed to be a buddy of the guy I was fighting with. He had a gun as well, although he did not pull it, he was not trying to hide it. Once again God was taking care of me, because for some reason I did not have a gun with me. This was very unusual, because I did not go anywhere without a gun. I certainly never robbed anyone without a gun. If I would have had my gun that whole situation would have gone badly. Most likely I would have lost my life that night, and would not be writing this today. Once everything calmed down the guys kept saying they were not cops. They wanted me to tell them who I got the dope from because that must have been who set me up. They said they would go with me and get the money back. At that point I knew with absolute certainty they were cops. I told them I did not know what they were talking about and I started to walk off. They arrested me and took me to jail. They had to release me after I served a 20-hour hold. They had to figure out what if anything they were going to be able to charge me with. They did not get any dope from me, and their money was gone. They were not sure what they could charge me with.

I knew they would be charging me with something, I just did not know what. This threw a wrench in my plan to go straight. I continued doing little things to make enough money to get by on. It wasn't long until the drug task force charged me with 'attempted distribution'. I was arrested and posted bond on the charge, plus I had to post a bond on a probation violation. My probation officer started the violation procedure when I got charged.

At that point I knew I was going to prison. Jennifer and I moved into my mom's house. Jennifer did not work or have any way to support herself, so I figured this would be the best place to leave her while I went and did my time. Once again, I had a good lawyer represent me and he got me a two year sentence that would be ran in with my first two year sentence. If I completed a 120-day shock program, they would let me out. Jennifer was four months pregnant at that time. I took the deal so I could be out before the baby was born. We said some tearful goodbye's then off to prison I went.

CHAPTER 5 – Coming Home

The 120-day shock consisted of an 84-day drug treatment program. If I completed the program my case would be sent back to the judge. He would decide if I would be released at that time, or go to another prison and serve my time. The program was rough. They spent more time making you be humble than they did retraining your mind to not desire drugs. The treatment took place in a section of Farmington prison. Most of the guards were from the prison and had no idea how to deal with addicts. They thought their job was to push us to the breaking point. If we snapped we would get kicked out of the program. What they did not realize was, it is easy to be humble when going home depends on your reaction. Something like 98% of the guys successfully completed the program, and 95% of them were back in prison within five years. This is the category I fall in. I completed the program and the judge let me go home on probation.

While I was in there my mom and Jennifer were unable to get along, so Jennifer went to stay with her dad in the city. By this time she was 8 months pregnant.

The prison was a long way from Kansas City, so I rode a Greyhound bus home. When I arrived at the bus depot in the city I found myself at a very important fork in the road. I had just spent 84 days being told everything I needed to do to stay sober. Now I was faced with my first big decision, who was I going to call to come get me? I could call my mom and go to her house where I had the best chance at staying drug free, or I could call my dad and go play the role of the big shot who just got out of prison. For some reason the people I ran with in the city saw going to prison as a badge of honor.

I had started going around my dad when I was 15 or 16. We had more of a friendship than father/son relationship. And to be honest we were not real good friends. We never did any of the regular father/son things. In fact the only thing we did together was get high on weed. I thought it was cool that I could get high with my dad. I am not sure what he thought. That night at the bus depot I made another of many bad decisions, I called my dad. I remember feeling so proud of myself sitting there in his living room. Everyone was treating me like I had really done something with myself. Then when my dad tried to pass me the joint and I told him no, I felt like I had just proved I was never going to smoke weed again. I was so full of foolish pride I could not hear the voice in my head screaming for me to get out of there and go home to my mom's house before it was too late.

I called Jennifer and told her to come and get me. She was there within minutes. I was so proud of myself for not getting high I decided I deserved a reward. On the way to her house we stopped at the liquor store so I could get a couple 40-ounces. I reasoned I had been gone for four months, so now it was time to celebrate a little. I don't think I made it through the first beer. The next morning I heard a horn out front. It was my Uncle Gary. He wanted to talk to me, so we went for a ride. He fired up a joint and I did not even act like I did not want it. The next thing I know I was stoned out of my mind and planning how I was going to get some money so I could get on my feet. Getting a job was no longer an option. All the great plans I had made while in the treatment center went out the window with that first joint.

Somehow I made it to my mom's house that day. When I walked through the door there was a moment of joy in her eyes, but it faded the second she saw my eyes. She knew I was stoned and she let me know just how she felt about it. Within a few days I was living back in the city with Jennifer.

I actually got a job and was working every day. Tom was a friend of my dad's, and he had a body shop. He hired me and was teaching me how to work on cars.

One day on my way to work I got pulled over and taken to jail on a bunch of traffic warrants. I think I had something like 15 outstanding traffic tickets. They ranged from two D.W.I.s to no seatbelt. As I said earlier, I had 9 D.W.I.s. I lost my license when I was 17, so every time I was pulled over I went to jail for driving without a license. My lawyer was at court the next morning and the judge was not letting me go. There would not be any fines this time; the judge wanted me to serve some time. I was sentenced to 90 days in Leeds (city jail). I had been released from prison on October 1, 1992, and I was in Leeds three weeks later.

After you had been there for a week you get in the work release program. I signed up and was allowed to leave 6 days a week. I left at 5:30 a.m. and did not have to be back until 8:00 p.m. I was allowed extra time because my job was so far from the jail. Since Tom was a friend and would not tell on me for not coming to work, I did not always make it to work. It was incredibly hard to walk into that jail every night. I made it a point to be stoned and I always made sure I had a shoe full of weed to share with a few buddies in there who were not able to get out. A buddy of mine was getting a ride from his sister-in-law every morning. He told me I could ride with them if I paid for the gas and smoked a joint with Stacy (his sister-in-law). After two days, she and I engaged in a sexual affair. She did not seem to mind that I had a pregnant girlfriend and that I was a scum bag, so I did not care either. Somehow I turned my time in Leeds into an every night party. Of course I was playing the role of Mr. Big Shot.

On November 6, 1992, after I dressed out to leave for the day, I was told I needed to call my mom's house. That morning I found out I had a little girl. I had Stacy drop me off at the hospital. I can't explain the overwhelming feeling of joy I felt when I picked that little girl up for the first time and held her in my arms. We named her Brittnie Diana. That was the happiest day of my life.

I was released from Leeds on January 2, 1993. Once again I found myself at a fork in the road. I was supposed to go to my mom's house when I got out. She was going to let me stay there while I got my life together. Well, there was one small problem; I did not have any weed. I had to make a pit stop at my dad's house to get a bag of weed before I went to my mom's. My mom and I fought all the time and there was no way I was going out there without some weed. I was stoned when I got to her house and once again she let me know how stupid she thought I was. After a couple days I ended up back in the city. Jennifer and I were staying with her dad. Then there was a gas leak in his house, so we went to my mom's. For some reason with the baby there, mom and I got along better.

Jennifer and I sat down and talked and we made up our minds it was time we grew up and took care of our baby. The truth is, she and my mom made it clear to me it was time for me to act like a man. Jennifer went to work at a nursing home and I went back to work at

Tom's shop. I was still getting high and drinking on the weekends. I always kept one foot in Satan's play ground. One night my mom and I went to pick Jennifer up at work and that was when I found out she had not been working there for a couple of weeks. Come to find out, after she was dropped off at work a guy named Mike would pick her up and they would go to Jennifer's dad's house. Then he would bring her back when it was time to get picked up. The night all of this came to light she packed her and the baby's things and we took her to her mom's house. The one request I had was for her not to take my baby to live with her dad.

There was a very good reason for this, but her dad is dead now so I will not speak ill of him.

We did not haggle over my visitation rights. I would get my daughter every other weekend plus any time I wanted her during the week. Two weeks later Jennifer moved out of her mom's house. She had taken my little girl and moved into a house which had been condemned by the city. She was staying there with Mike and a group of people. I almost lost my mind when I found out the conditions my daughter was living in. Jennifer decided she was not going to let me see my daughter any more. I wanted to go and do something very bad to her and everyone else in that house, but my mom talked some sense into me. She got Jennifer to bring Brittnie to our house to visit my grandma who was in from Oregon.

When Jennifer showed up at the house, she was spun out on speed. This was new. While we were together she rarely smoked pot. After Jennifer left, my mom examined the baby and found she was in immediate need of medical attention. Brittnie was only eating 2 ounces of formula a day and had been using her pacifier as a food supplement. Malnutrition caused her to have a deep indention in the roof of her mouth, and she had a severe ear infection. I have never been so angry in my life. My mom and Reno knew I was going to do something real bad, so they refused to let me leave the house. Mom said she would help me get custody of Brittnie, and she would help me take care of her. The only condition was I had to do everything 100% legally.

When she came to pick up Brittnie I informed her I had gotten an ex parte order of protection against her and she could not leave the house with the baby. With the doctor's statement, the order was given without question. I was doing everything in my power to stay calm. I told her we needed to talk about what was best for Brittnie. Jennifer did not want to talk. She ran out of the house screaming. After she calmed down, she came back and her and my mom and I sat down and talked. We all decided the best place for Brittnie was at my mom's house. It was made clear that Jennifer and I could come there and spend all the time we wanted with Brittnie. Neither one of us were allowed leave the house with Brittnie. We had to sign papers giving my mom full parental rights. This was done to get insurance, and to assure neither Jennifer or I popped up one day and decided to take the baby. The papers we signed stated if either one of us got our lives together and could establish we were living responsible lives we could get our child and my mom would not contest us.

The day after we left the lawyer's office, Jennifer went and saw Brittnie four times. Then she did not come by any more. She has called to check on Brittnie three or four times in the last 19 years. My mom has raised Brittnie as if she were her own child.

CHAPTER 6 – Crystal Returns

I went back to my mom's to live. My goal was to settle down and take care of Brittnie. I thought getting away from the city would help me keep my head on straight. I worked a few jobs, but I never stayed at any of them for long. My life still revolved around partying. It is hard to make it to work after staying out all night drinking.

To my surprise many of the guys I knew from my mom's neighborhood had started using crystal meth. My mom lives in Independence, a suburb of Kansas City, and at that time Independence was known as the Meth Capital of the United States. It did not take me long to start using meth myself.

Although I had used it a few times when I lived in

California, I had yet to have the true meth experience. Meth is a drug that lures you in and before you know it you are addicted beyond belief. When meth got into my system I became a different person. I pretended like I still cared about doing well and taking care of my daughter, but just under the surface the only thing I could think about was dope.

Since I knew a lot of people it only made sense for me to start selling meth. I moved out of my mom's house. Even as messed up as my head was I knew I could never risk dragging any drama home to my mom and daughter.

I remember standing in my mom's kitchen a few months after I moved out. My throat was so sore I could barely swallow. You could almost count my teeth without me having to open my mouth. I was standing there telling her I was not using anything. The signs of an addict are incredibly obvious to everybody except the user. A person will stand there with white powder all around their nose and swear by God and everything they love, they are not using. I believe crystal meth is made up of billions of little demons. Users pump them demons into their bodies one granular at a time. It is a form of self-induced demonic possession. Once your body gets full of those little demons, all you can think about is how you are going to get more of them.

While a person is under the spell of meth they have no friends or family. Whether everyone is really out to get you or not, you believe everyone is your enemy. When I was selling meth, I would set up shop at a friend's house. I would get them high for letting me use their house. There were times I would go a week or longer without sleeping. Lack of sleep on this scale causes the human mind to start hallucinating. Before long you are no longer able to tell the difference between reality and the hallucinations.

After I had pushed my body to the limit I would get a hotel room somewhere so I could crash. Often I could sleep for a couple days. When I came to I would have to sit there and try to sort out my memories, trying to figure out what all had happened the previous week or so. These brief moments of sobriety were when I would go to my mom's and visit with Brittnie. My mom would beg me to stay there and stop living the life I was living. I think she was more worried about me at that time than she was when I was running with them brothers from the neighborhood. I always told her I had one more thing to do then I would come home. For a meth addict, that "one more thing" never gets done.

Around September of 1993, a friend of mine introduced me to a woman named Laura. She was from the neighborhood and liked getting high as much as I did. Neither of us used needles, so we thought we were meant for each other. I have done dope every way possible except injecting it. God blessed me with a fear of needles that no amount of dope could overcome.

Laura and I had a real nice apartment. She was stripping, and I was selling dope hand over fist. Between our incomes we never needed money, and the dope flowed freely through our apartment. When it was time to crash we would bar the door and no one would hear from us for a couple days. This went on for months.

It was not long until it seemed like we were arguing all the time. One of us would get spun out and snap out on the other for no apparent reason. I could not count the pieces of furniture that got broken during these fits. One time I even managed to break our king size bed in half. Laura would get mad and start hitting me with everything she could get her hands on, and I would grab her and hold her down until we both calmed down. This type of relationship was not new to me. I had watched my mom and Bubba have this same type of relationship for the first 13 years of my life. I always swore I would never follow their example, but here I was living the same way they did. Only Laura and I were meth addicts and literally out of our minds more often than not.

We would fight, split up, then get back together. This was an ongoing pattern for about a year. We both finally had enough of this merry-go-round, so we split up for what we thought was for good. A buddy and I got a house in Independence. We were both addicts, but had both decided to get jobs and leave the dope alone. I went to work for a roofing company. I set a goal to learn how to roof houses and then start my own roofing business. I did the research and discovered it did not take very much capital to start a roofing business. I had enough connections in the real-estate business I would be able to have plenty of work.

I had been working for a couple of months when I got a message from Laura saying it was important I get a hold of her. At first I did not call her back, but after about 20 messages I called her back and she told me she was pregnant with my child. She told me she had quit stripping and was working for a telemarketing company. We decided the best thing we could do was give our relationship one more try. Everyone in her family and my family told us we were crazy to get back together. I moved back to the neighborhood in an apartment with her. I ask her to marry me and she said yes. I started my own roofing business and things were looking good.

Laura was staying clean, with the exception of taking a hit off a joint every once in a while. I was leaving the meth alone but was still smoking pot, and had started eating Xanax. I was eating about 90 of them a week. To be honest I am not sure which drug is more dangerous, Xanax or meth. When I would mix alcohol with Xanax, I became a different person. This mixture often caused me to become violent beyond control. After every bad episode I swore to make it a point not to drink while taking Xanex. But being an addict, I always pushed the limits of everything I did. This was a pattern in my life, everything I did, I did it to the extreme limits.

One day while I was cleaning the apartment I found some paper work that stated Laura was to testify on a case that involved an escort service. This sent my head spinning. After a few phone calls I found out while Laura and I were split up she had gone to work for an escort service. While working there the place had been busted for prostitution. The people I talked to were unable to tell me exactly what Laura's role was in the company.

I had just picked up 90 pills that day. This seemed like a good time to start eating them. All that day I dwelled on the information I had received. I had to ask Laura about it, but I did not know how to bring it up. For some reason I really was not mad at her, I just wanted to figure out a way for her to get out of the mess she had gotten herself into. My thought was; if something happened to the guy who was running the company then her problem would go away. Something in my head told me maybe a couple beers would help me figure this mess out.

When Laura came home that day I did not say anything to her about what I had found out. I just continued to drink beer, and eat Xanax. That night we dropped her daughter off at her aunt's house and went to the lake. We were going to go fishing, but when we got there it was too chilly for her so we turned around and headed home. I stopped at a liquor store and bought a 5th of Crown Royal. When I got in the car I opened it and started drinking it like it was water.

The next thing I remember is Laura and I were back at the apartment and I was confronting her with the information I got that day. At first she denied everything, but then when I showed her the paper work I had found, she got mad at me. I can still hear that little voice in my head telling me to get out of there, but I was unable to obey it. At the climax of our argument Laura told me she had in fact been working at the escort service and she had turned tricks. The last thing she said to me was the baby she was carrying might belong to one of the guys she was with. At that point something inside of me snapped and I went into a fit of rage. For the first time in my life I doubled up my fist and hit a woman, not once but three times. I am told Laura had marks on her neck, but I do not remember choking her. I got up and unhooked the phone, grabbed her purse and car keys and I left. She had called the police on me before when we argued so I knew she was going to call them over this and I wanted a head-start out of there before she could call them.

I drove to my mom's house and I passed out on the couch. The next morning I had a roofing job to finish so I had my little cousin go help me. After we finished it we went to my apartment. I told him if Laura called the police to get out of there. When I went in the apartment

I felt something was wrong.

Then when I turned the corner to our bedroom my worst nightmare came true. Laura was still lying in the same spot, and it was obvious she was dead.

I told my cousin to call the police, something bad had happened. He could not find the phone; I forgot I had taken it the night before. I told him to go to the neighbors and use their phone. I stayed there until the police arrived. Being the boyfriend, and having a criminal record, I was the first one they suspected, so they took me in for a 20-hour hold. I made up a story about leaving her at home and going to the lake without her. I told them I did not know what happened to her. They let me go after 20 hours.

A couple days after this happened one of the brothers I use to run with called me with a roofing job. He came and picked me up. He told me he had heard about what happened to Laura. We talked for about an hour. I did not want to tell him I accidently killed her, so I told a story that made me sound like a real criminal. Once again, I was trying to impress my old partner in crime. What I did not know was my partner in crime was an informant for the F.B.I., and he was wearing a wire on me.

CHAPTER 7 – 2 Counts of 1st Degree Murder

A couple days after my conversation with my former partner who was now an F.B.I. informant, I was arrested and charged with 2 counts of first degree murder and they were seeking the death penalty in my case. The first count was on Laura, and count two was on our baby she was carrying. I did not find out until later that the baby was mine. It is impossible for me to put into words the emotions I felt at that time. It took years for me to completely process what I had done. After my arrest I had to deal with being told I was never going to see the outside world again. Every moment of the first two or three months in the county jail was spent with my mind racing trying to figure out what I had to do so I could get out of the mess I had gotten myself into.

My mom hired a lawyer for me. His name was Gerry Jaco, and at that time he was on a hot streak in Jackson County Missouri. He had beaten three murder cases in the previous year. I felt as though I had found my savior. When he came to see me, he told me he was not interested in whether or not I had committed the crime. He told me his job was to get me acquitted and that is what he was going to do. That was music to my ears. This man had just told me exactly what I wanted to hear. Time after time I tried to tell him what really happened that night, but he would always cut me off. He told me we were going to stick with the original story I told the police when they took me in for the 20-hour hold. I felt like my crime was not first degree murder. I did not plan to kill Laura that night. The thought of killing her had never gone through my mind. I did not even know she was dead when I left the house that night. I really wanted to tell the court what really happened. I knew telling the truth was not going to get me sent home, but it would show the court my crime was not first degree murder. Mr. Jaco would not hear it. We were doing things his way.

About this time I started reading my Bible. This was a pattern every time I got in trouble. Once I got comfortable in whatever place of confinement I found myself, I would become a Bible reading Christian. I always had this unexplainable force pulling me to the Scriptures. The problem with my form of Christianity was I tended to focus on the verses that said stuff like, *"And all things, whatsoever ye shall ask in prayer believing, ye shall receive."* (Matthew 21:22)

I was certainly praying for God to let me out of jail. I believed with all my heart of stone that he could do it. According to His Word He HAD to give me what I wanted, right? I made it a point to avoid all the verses that tell us He will give us everything we ask as long as it is in His will. This mistake was just like the mistake I made by asking Jesus to be the Lord of my life, then trying to turn the Creator of Heaven and Earth and all things which dwell therein into my personal get-out-of-jail-free card. The whole time I was sitting in the county jail my favorite story in the Bible was, *"But the angel of the Lord by night opened the prison doors, and brought them forth, and said, Go stand and speak in the temple to the people all the words of this life."* (Acts 5:19-20)

My whole walk with God was based on the idea He was going to work with my lawyer and let me beat my case. Then allow me to be released back into the world so I could go preach for Him. My whole perception of what it meant to be a Christian was wrong. They had people who came to the county jail and preach to us. The problem was most of them were preaching a "name it and claim it" message. This is a very false and dangerous message to preach to anyone, much less someone facing prison time. At the time it sounded good and I bought into it hook, line, and sinker.

My lawyer had the court order for me to have a mental examination. This was standard procedure in a murder trial. When I went to see the doctors I had this overwhelming desire to tell them the truth about what happened that night. Up to that point I had not told anyone what really happened. I went in and unloaded the truth on the doctors. I felt like a ton of bricks had been taken off my chest that day. When I told my lawyer what I had done he was furious. He called my mom to his office and told her if I went to trial and told them the story I told the doctors I would most certainly get the death penalty. He threatened to step off my case and leave me to the Public Defender system. My mom told him she did not have the money to get another attorney. That was when Mr. Gerry Jaco told her if she did not find a way to get him $10,000.00 dollars he was going to step off my case. Yes, he blackmailed my mom. My mom and grandma came up with the money and I was told by Mr. Jaco I would be sticking to my original story or he would not represent me. Once again he assured me he was going to beat my case.

A couple years after my trial Mr. Jaco was disbarred by the Missouri Bar Association because of his unethical practices in other client's cases; he is no longer able to practice law anywhere. Today he runs a house painting business in another state.

A few months before my trial, the state dropped the death penalty. On February 14, 1995, I went to trial, and against my better judgment I took the stand and testified to the original lie I had told the police. Plus, at the guidance of Mr. Jaco, I added a few totally unbelievable parts to my story. Looking back, that jury must have thought I was the dumbest guy in the world to sit there and tell them the stuff that came out of my mouth that day. At one point my trial had to be stopped by the court. The jury was removed from the courtroom and the judge read me my rights. My own lawyer had led me down a line of questioning that put me at risk of admitting to a crime that carried the same punishment as the one I was on trial for. When the jury was brought back in the courtroom I had to recant my statements that I had just made in front of them. The only problem with recanting a statement is there is no way to ever unspeak a spoken word. I could tell by the look on the juror's faces, my trial was done. They did not hear anything that was said in that courtroom for the next two days.

It did not come as a surprise to me when after 6 hours of deliberation, the jury came back with a guilty verdict. The whole time my trial was going on I knew I was supposed to take the stand and tell those people the truth about what happened that night. My failure to listen to the Spirit speaking to me got me convicted of 2 counts of first degree murder. Count one was on Laura, and count two was on our baby she was carrying. At that time I wished they would have put the death penalty back on the table because that is what I wanted. What I did not want was to spend the rest of my life in prison. I still thought I deserved mercy from the court. Regardless of what I thought, God had other plans for my life.

I had to wait 30 days for my sentencing date. The only

thing the court could give me was two life sentences without the possibility of parole.

Three days after I was sentenced I was transferred to Fulton Diagnostic Center, and my life in prison started.

CHAPTER 8 – Prison Life

The razor-wire fences I saw when I arrived at Fulton were the most depressing thing I had ever laid eyes on. I knew in my mind the rest of my life would be spent behind fences like a caged animal. Who was I to complain though? I lived like an animal, now the state was treating me like one.

The first thing they do when a person arrives is begin the dehumanization process. They stripped me naked then placed me in a room with around 150 other naked men. Next I was sent to a window where I was sprayed with lice spray. The officer did his best to humiliate everyone that came to his spray station. After I was thoroughly debugged, I was sent to the shower. After that I was given underwear and a jumpsuit that was three sizes too big. A person would much rather have it too big rather than too little. After I had my picture taken, a number was assigned to me. 514068 became my new last name. I was then sent to a housing unit where, due to overcrowding I was given a cot in the dayroom.

Each wing had an inmate worker who gave new guys soap and toilet paper when they arrived in the wing. This guy also had access to the roster that showed how much time a person was doing, and whether or not they were sex offenders. An odd thing happened when I got in the wing. It seemed everyone was eager to help me out with smokes and coffee. I immediately went on the defensive. I thought there were ulterior motives behind this unusual kindness.

Come to find out the wing worker "Scooter" had told some of the 'cool guys' I was life without parole (LWOP). This gave a person a certain level of respect.

I only had to spend one night on the cot. The next day I was moved to a cell. My first celly was a guy named Steve Ragen. He was a few years younger than me, but we got along great. He was serving life and 20, so we were both dealing with the knowledge that we were probably going to die in prison. After spending 23 hours a day in that cell for four months we established a true friendship. A person does not make a lot of friends in this world, let alone in prison, but Steve was a true friend.

It was while I was at Fulton a woman named Marcia and I began having a romantic relationship. Marcia was a friend of my mom's. She started working for my mom when I was 15 or 16. We use to play around a lot, but were never romantically involved until I came to prison. I truly loved her, and she loved me. It is hard to explain how two people from such different backgrounds could fall in love, but we did. Our relationship lasted 14 years.

Steve left Fulton and went to Missouri State Penitentiary (MSP). A few months later I was sent to Potosi Correctional Center. Potosi was where they sent death-row inmates and LWOP's.

I quickly found out a person could get drugs pretty freely in prison. In fact sometimes it was easier to get drugs in prison than it was on the streets. It was not long until I came across another inmate who was moving drugs into the prison. He had the way to get it in, and I still had a few of my connections on the streets. It was not long until my life was consumed with staying high.

That empty place in my heart I told you about earlier had grown from a hole, to something that made the Grand Canyon look like a dimple on an orange. Although the drugs did not fill the void, they did make my brain so numb I was often able to block out the void.

One thing I found out about the dope game in prison is you have no friends. The level of jealously guys have toward the movers is unbelievable. It did not take long until I found myself doing my first of many long stretches in "the hole." Another inmate had gotten beat up badly and my celly and I found ourselves in the hole. I ended up getting transferred to MSP after serving eight months in the hole.

I thought going to MSP was going to be a good thing. I knew a lot of guys from the neighborhood were there, and my buddy Steve was there. MSP is the oldest prison west of the Mississippi. It was built in 1820 as a territorial prison. Upon arriving at MSP I was taken through an old iron bar door. This was the same door cowboys had once been taken through. The moment I entered that place the presence of evil was so thick it entered every pore on my body. I quickly realized I had just entered another realm, separate from the world that existed outside the iron door.

It did not take long for me to fall into the dope game. My life became consumed with prison life. My time was spent getting high, lifting weights, playing basketball, or handball. I did not have anything good in my life. At that time my buddy Steve was into a pagan religion which was motivated by racism. This seemed like something I wanted to be part of. It was not long until I completely turned my back on God and hung a wooden hammer around my neck. I really did not believe in the pagan gods, I just did it to fit in with the crowd.

It was not long until I was in the hole again. A man has plenty of time to think while being locked in a cage alone for 23 hours a day. While I was in the hole God spoke to my heart and I decided I did not want to have anything to do with paganism any more. I told God He was the only one I would worship. I believed faith in Jesus is the only means of salvation. I believed, but I was not ready to make Jesus the Lord of my life. Drugs were the lord of my life.

In 1997 they opened a maximum security prison in Cameron, Missouri. Cameron is about 45 minutes from my mom and Brittnie. They were taking volunteers, so I signed up. I had only had two visits while at MSP. It was too far for my mom to drive on a regular basis. I figured I would be able to get more visits at the new prison. Plus I was ready to get out of MSP.

You could not imagine how nasty that place was. Men had to put cotton in their ears at night to keep the cockroaches from crawling in there and laying eggs. And the rats were big enough to carry off a bag of potato-chips.

They named the new prison Crossroads Correctional Center. When we opened this place it was completely out of control. The guards hired to work here were not ready for the level of drugs and violence they were responsible for dealing with. At one point Crossroads was deemed the most dangerous prison in the United States. That was when administration locked the prison down. We were only allowed out of our cells for 20 minutes to shower and use the phone three times a day.

Only one house was allowed on the recreation yard at a time, and only for an hour period four times a week. After a while the violence slowed down greatly, but the drug traffic did not slow down at all. I was in and out of the hole regularly. All my trips to the hole were drug related in one form or another. I spent eight out of my first fourteen years in the hole.

Up to this point the only drugs I did was smoke pot and eat downers. I was not interested in the hard drugs. That all changed in 2003 when I went to another new prison they opened in Charleston, Missouri. I was getting tired of Crossroads and they were taking volunteers so Toney and I signed up to go down there. Up to this point Toney and Steve were the only two people I considered my friends. Once I got down there I found the drugs were even more plentiful than they had been at Crossroads. They were also much cheaper.

This is when I got introduced to heroin. I had never done it before because I thought the only way to do it was to inject it, and I was not going to poke a needle in my body. A guy I was running with showed me how to snort it. I was hooked immediately. I had never experienced a high like that before. It was not long until I had a habit. I was getting high pretty much every day on one thing or another, usually heroin.

Charleston was so far from home I was not getting any visits, and I had honestly reached a point in life where I did not care whether I lived or died. I never actually tried to kill myself, but on more than one occasion I did enough heroin to kill two or three people. My attitude led me to push the limits on everything I did. I would mix crack, weed, heroin, and Klonopin. This was a very deadly mixture not many people came back from. The whole time I was doing this, those around me could not figure out how I was still alive, and to be honest neither could I. What I did not know at the time was, God had a plan for my life which was yet to be fulfilled.

I ended up going to the hole after I got caught with some dope in my sock. I did eight months in the hole for possession. The whole time I was in the hole the only book I read was the Bible. I knew I needed to change my life. I knew God was the only one for me to turn to. Once again the problem was I did not want to make Jesus the Lord of my life, I wanted to retain my sense of control. Once again, I was trying to con God.

My goal when I got out of the hole was not to get high any more. Yet, I found myself sitting in my cell stoned out of my mind in less than 24 hours. I told myself I could smoke pot but I had to leave heroin alone. Well, it was not long until I was using even more than before. I got to the point where I was seriously thinking about using a needle. I wanted to get higher and that was the only way to do it. Before I went that far I told Toney I was going to the hole and going to make them transfer me back to Crossroads. I had to get closer to home so I could see my little girl, before my little girl was burying her dad.

I spent 70 days in the hole and was sent back to Crossroads. I fell right back into my pattern of using drugs, going to the hole, then swearing I would never do it again. This pattern continued until 2007. I had stopped doing heroin and was only smoking pot every once in a while. I had acted good long enough to be admitted in the honor dorm. This meant I was not locked down except for count and at night. I was getting to see my daughter and mom on a fairly regular basis. I had managed to stay out of the hole for a little over two years. This was a record for me.

I was quite proud of myself, I had quit doing heroin all on my own. People always talk about how hard it is to kick heroin. I proved them all wrong because I had quit without any help. This gave me a level of false pride that was unmeasurable by human standards. Then Satan broke out his ruler in the form of a guy I knew coming and making me an unbelievable deal on a very large piece of heroin. There was no way I could pass up this deal. My initial thought was I could sell it in pieces and make almost $500.00. Due to the great deal I got on the dope, I decided I had better test it to make sure it was good before I sold it to anyone. I told myself it would be alright since all I needed to do was a little piece to tell me if it was any good or not.

I sat down and cut off a little piece and snorted it, I didn't feel anything. Maybe I did not do enough, so I cut off another piece. Over about a 4 hour period I managed to snort over half a gram of heroin. I am not sure what happened. I did not mean to keep snorting it. The only thing I can figure out is I got so high I blacked out and just kept snorting the dope. This was way too much dope for any one person to ingest. The last thing I remembered was cleaning up my mess, then getting up in my bed and lying down to watch some T.V. At some point my lungs shut down and I died. When my celly came back in the cell he noticed I was not breathing and had turned blue. He went and told the guards something was wrong with me and I needed help. He did not get high, and had no idea what was wrong with me. When the nurses and guards carried me out of the cell they had pronounced me dead and pulled a sheet over my head.

At this point in my life I truly thought I was saved. If someone would have asked me where I thought I would go if I died, I would have told them without a doubt heaven. While I was dead I found out I was wrong. All I remember is crying out to God, but in my spirit I felt He was not listening to me. I felt myself surrounded in a blackness that cannot be explained with words. I felt like I was completely alone and drifting into deeper blackness.

All I could do was cry out to God and ask Him to please give me one more chance at life. I have been in some pretty frightening situations in my life, but nothing I have ever felt in the flesh compares to the fear I experienced in my spirit that night. I knew without a doubt I was going to hell. To my great relief, God was not done with me yet. When they got my body to medical, one of the nurses (Gary) went to work on me trying to see if he could get a pulse. God used that man to beat life back into my dead body. Once he got a light pulse Gary kept working me until the ambulance arrived. The paramedics injected me with a chemical called "Narcan." This drug reverses the effects of heroin and brought me all the way back from the dead. When I came to in the ambulance the first thought that went through my mind was "Thank you God." I laid in the hospital for three days thinking about what had happened to me. The one thing I knew for sure was I had to reevaluate my thoughts on what it meant to be saved from the fires of hell, because what I thought I knew was wrong.

PART TWO

"Therefore if any man be in Christ, he is a new creature: old things are passed away; behold all things are become new."

(2 Corinthians 5:17)

CHAPTER 9 – A New Beginning

When I was released from the hospital and returned to the prison, I was placed in Administrative Segregation for 30 days. This was so they could investigate what had happened to me. All the drugs were out of my system by the time they did a drug test on me, so they were not able to give me a conduct violation. After being released from the hole I was placed back in the honor dorm. While I was in the hole I spent my time reading the Bible.

Only this time it was different. I knew I had to take what I was reading out to the yard with me. Now I was searching to find out what it means to be saved. I prayed for God to show me where I had gone wrong with my thinking on Salvation. It was during this time

God enlightened me to what Jesus meant when He said:

> *"Not everyone that saith unto me, Lord, Lord, shall enter into the kingdom of heaven; but he that doeth the will of my Father which is in heaven. Many will say to me in that day, Lord, Lord, have we not prophesied in thy name? and in thy name have cast out devils? and in thy name done many wonderful works? And then will I profess unto them, I never knew you: depart from me, ye that work iniquity."*

(Matthew 7:21-23)

This verse sends a chill down my spine every time I read it now. For years I had read the Bible and somehow I missed what Jesus was saying here. Just because a person claims to be saved and a child of God doesn't necessarily mean they are. Being saved does not take place in our head or in our speech; it takes place in our heart. When a person has been saved by the blood of Jesus they are given a new heart, and their desire in life is to walk as Jesus walked and to do the will of the Father.

The Holy Spirit opened my eyes to the knowledge that I had to make Jesus the Lord of my life. To make Jesus the Lord of my life meant I could no longer live according to my will, but I had to seek God's will in every situation I faced for the rest of my life. It did not take me very long to figure out this was a lot harder to do than say. To be honest I thought it was impossible at first, and I seemed to fail every time I turned around. As the years have passed it has become a little easier to submit to God's will. I still have numerous struggles, but I am learning to lean on God and not myself during times of struggles.

Before I go any further let me say, I am 100% certain that the Bible is clear that we are saved by grace through faith, and our works are a result of our Salvation:

> *"For by grace are ye saved through faith; and that not of yourselves: it is the gift of God: Not of works least any man should boast. For we are His workmanship, created in Christ Jesus unto good works, which God hath before ordained that we should walk in them."*

(Ephesians 2:8-10)

No amount of good works or obeying the law can ever earn a person Salvation. Being saved is not based on how many times a person goes to church, or how 'good' they are. Salvation was bought for us by Jesus Christ. He took our rightful place on the cross, and paid our sin debt. Salvation is not earned. We are told it is given freely when:

"That if thou shalt confess with thy mouth the Lord Jesus, and shalt believe in thy heart that God hath raised Him from the dead, thou shalt be saved. Forwith the heart man believeth unto righteousness; and with the mouth confession is made unto salvation."

(Romans 10:9-10)

Before I died I thought I knew and understood these seemingly simple verses. Every time I had gone to a church service the preacher quoted this verse and told us to come forward and we would be saved from the fires of hell. Thank God I was given the opportunity to come back and find out where I had erred. I now know there was a lot more to these verses than I thought. I had read the Bible literally hundreds of times in my life.

I knew what it said, but I did not know what it meant. The first thing I did when I got out of the hole was go to the library and find a book on how to study the Bible. I found a book called "How to Study the Bible" by Tim Lahaye. He is the guy that wrote the "Left Behind" books. It was him who taught me there was much more to studying the Bible than just reading it. His book is where I learned I need to get some very important tools to help me study the Bible thoroughly. The first thing I needed was a Exhaustive Concordance. A fellow Christian told me the best one to get was "The Strongest Strongs." This concordance lists every word in the Bible every time it is used and where it can be found. This is an awesome tool. Any time I can't remember where a verse is, all I have to do is look up a word in the verse and I find what I am looking for. This is also an excellent help when doing a word study.

If you are studying the word 'faith' you can look it up and see every time it is used in the Bible. The next tool I needed was a good Bible dictionary. The Bible I have is numbered to Strong's numbering system so I went with the "The Complete Word Study Dictionary, New Testament" and the "The Complete Word Study Dictionary, Old Testament." In Strong's numbering system every word in the Bible has a number. This number will take you to the meaning in the dictionaries. Some words have multiple meanings. This system allows a person to look up how the word is used in the particular verse they are reading. I also needed a commentary, so I went with "The MacArthur Bible Commentary." A commentary is someone else teaching you what the Scriptures mean. It is essential to be able to seek wisdom from those who are smarter than yourself. John MacArthur is a very trusted Bible scholar, and I recommend his commentary to every student of the Bible. Now that I had my tools it was time for me to start searching the Scriptures to find out where I had erred in my thoughts on Salvation.

The first place I went back to was (Romans 10:9) where we are told that as long as we "believe" we will be saved. I did a word study on the word "believe" and came across a verse that troubled me greatly:

> *"Thou believest there is one God; thou doest well: the devils also believe and tremble."*

(James 2:19)

This told me there had to be more to the words

"believe" and "confess" than I had been taught. I found my answer in John MacArthur's 'Bible Commentary'. He says: This is "not a simple acknowledgment that He is God and the Lord of the universe, since even demons acknowledge that to be true (James 2:19). This is the deep personal conviction, without reservation, that Jesus is that person's own master sovereign. This phrase includes repenting from sin, trusting in Jesus for salvation, and submitting to Him as Lord. This is the volitional [exercising of the will] element of faith."

The 'Word Study Dictionary' says: "Belief creates complete dependence upon the Lord and not independence." Now I was beginning to understand where I had gone wrong in my thinking. Not only had I never truly repented from my sins, I had certainly never made Jesus the unconditional Lord of my life. Sure, when I got caught doing wrong I would ask God to forgive me. This was always followed up by a request of leniency. Then I would often go out and willingly do the same thing again. To repent means to turn from sin and not willfully do it again. Although I believed, I most certainly had never made Jesus the Lord of my life. I was my own lord and my fleshly desires were all I served. These two key elements of Salvation were not part of my life. Looking back I see how vain I was to think I could just tell Jesus I believed in Him and wanted Him to take me to heaven when I died, but as long as I was on the earth I was going to live how I wanted to.

Thank God for second chances. It was at this point I realized I had to ask Jesus to be the Lord of my life and to teach me His will for my life. I finally surrendered my life to Jesus and told Him I wanted to serve Him for the rest of my time on earth. That was the moment Salvation came into my heart, and I became a new creature. As a new creature in Jesus I had to learn how to live for Him. I would like to tell you that from that moment on I never sinned again and have lived a perfect life, but that is not the case for me, or anyone who becomes a Christian. It was at that moment the greatest war ever fought began in my heart. This is the war that goes on in every person the moment they become a Christian. The flesh goes to war against the Spirit:

> *"For the flesh lusteth against the Spirit, and the Spirit against the flesh: and these are contrary the one to the other: so you cannot do the things that ye would."* (Galatians 5:17)

This is a war Christians will fight until the day their bodies of flesh die and their soul goes to be with Jesus for all eternity. When we fail and find ourselves sinking in the troubles of the world, and we find we are not walking in the Spirit, we must cry out to Jesus like Peter cried out to when he started to sink (Matthew 14:30-31). When we cry out, Jesus will reach out and pick us up and place us back behind Him on the battle field. It did not take me long to figure out I had no idea what it meant to walk in the Spirit and not the flesh. I needed to prayerfully search the Bible to learn how a Christian is to walk in the Spirit and resist the desires of the flesh.

CHAPTER 10 – Learning to Love

Before I started my walk with Jesus, love was something I reserved for immediate family. On the surface I think I loved some of the women I was with romantically. I never surrendered my whole heart to anyone. I always equated love with trust. I learned at a very young age trusting people was not something you did. My unwillingness to trust people caused me to never truly love anyone in the purest sense of the word. Scripture commands me to overcome my fear of loving others when Jesus says,

> *"A new commandment I give unto you, that ye love one another; as I have loved you, that ye also love one another. By this ye shall know that ye are my*

disciples, if ye love one another."

(John 13:34-35)

Here Jesus commands me to love others as He loves me. This tells me I have to put all of my fears aside and love people unconditionally. Trusting people has nothing to do with loving them. If Jesus would have waited until He trusted me to love me I would have never experienced His love. Jesus loved the very people who were driving nails into His hands pinning Him to a wooden cross.

I cannot tell you how many people I have said, "'I love you" to, then as soon as something went wrong in the relationship and we parted ways I stopped loving them. This tells me my love for them was conditional and very shallow. I would like to say family is different, but it really isn't.

I have a few family members who I believe have done me wrong. I have some love for them, but it is not the same kind of love Jesus has for me. Jesus tells me this way of loving them has to change.

When I began to study the Scripture on the subject of love I noticed a recurring theme. Jesus loves me no matter what I have done, or what I will do. Nothing I do surprises Him. He knew my every move before He set the foundation of the world in place and He still chose to love me. One of the most comforting Scriptures in the Bible is,

> *"God commendeth His love toward us, in that while we were yet sinners, Christ died for us."*

(Romans 5:8)

Even when every fiber of my body was engulfed in the sins of this world, Jesus loved me. His love for me is not shallow, it is so deep He allowed Himself to be tortured and murdered to pay the price for my sin. Now He commands me to love others the same way. Not only am I commanded by my Lord and Savior to love those whom I call friends and family, He tells me I am to love all people, even my enemies,

> *"But I say unto you, Love your enemies, bless them that curse you, do good to them that hate you, and pray for them which despitefully use you, and persecute you; That ye may be the*

> *children of your Father which is in heaven: for He maketh His sun to rise on the evil and on the good, and sendeth rain on the just and the unjust."*

(Matthew 5:44-45)

When I first began to understand what this verse was telling me to do, I told God "I can't do this, you are asking too much." My hate for certain people runs way too deep for me to ever be able to love them. God told me that to be His child meant I would spend every moment of the rest of my life doing my best to obey this commandment. As a child of God, the duty is mine, but the power to love comes from God. No matter how many times I have failed to love, when I call on Jesus, He picks me up and I try again. Truly loving others is the hardest thing I have ever done in my life. I spent the first 34 years of my life hating people, and to be honest it was pretty easy to do.

When I first began to try to obey this commandment God gave me a glimpse of how much hate I had in my heart. My childhood was spent hating my step dad, and all the people who allowed him to treat me and my mom the way he did. In my teen years I think I hated myself as well as the world. This hatred led to a life of self-destruction, and destruction of others. I have now spent my entire adult life in a maximum security prison where hating is second only to breathing.

When I started examining all the hate in my heart I was surprised at what I found. I made a list of everyone I hated and why I hated them. I realized I hated the correction officers because they were doing their job.

I hated the guy next door to me because he was black. I did not know anything about him. Yet, I spent a lot of time hating him and everyone who looked like him. I hated a whole table full of guys because they slammed the dominoes while I was trying to take a nap. I hated my celly because he snored at night. I am amazed at how easy it is to hate another one of God's creatures. Hate is like a bad case of the Chicken Pox, the more you scratch it the more it spreads until your whole body is covered with the virus. God is the only medicine that stops the spread and soothes the sores hate causes.

While I was making my list of people I hated, the Holy Spirit revealed to me that most of the people I hated had never personally done anything to me. I hated them because that is what I had spent my life programming myself to do. Hating them was a lot easier than looking inside myself where I might find the real problem was me. I started praying for God to bring it to my attention the moment I let hate for another person enter my mind. Hate is something I had to cut off at the mind before it made its way to my heart. God is faithful to get my attention when I err. At first my days were consumed with praying for forgiveness. I think every time I turned around I was finding hate creeping up in my mind. Over the years it has gotten a little easier. I still struggle with it every day of my life. I have to rely on God to keep a close watch on my emotions or I find myself starting to hate people for the dumbest reasons. God has taught me the importance of repenting immediately when He makes me aware of my sin.

A preacher gave us a sermon one time telling us that we must find a reason to love everyone. I felt like he was speaking directly to me. He told me when I felt the desire to hate someone I had to find a reason to love them. I almost giggled when he said, "Everyone has something about them to love." I wanted to ask him if he knew where I lived. Then he said something that I will never forget. He said, "If you can't find anything about them personally to love, love them because they are God's children and He told you to love them." In this one sentence the preacher took away every one of my excuses for not loving certain people. It is through the power of the Holy Spirit I no longer desire to hate others. The sin of hate still raises its ugly head and attacks me, but I am learning to rid it from my life before it takes root in my heart. An amazing thing has happened to me. I have learned it is easier and healthier to love others than it is to hate them.

Learning to love those around me was just the first step. Now I had to learn to love those who I thought I had very good reason to hate. I asked God if I was really supposed to love Bubba? Was I supposed to love the guy that told on me and got me locked up for the rest of my life? Of everyone that had wronged me in my life these two stood out the most in my heart. My hate for these two men was so strong I could feel it pumping through my veins. I often spent nights awake thinking of horrible ways I wanted to pay them back for what they had done to me. Loving these two men was something I was not sure I would ever be able to do. Then God used a verse in the Bible to change feelings toward these two men whom I hated so much,

> *"If any man say, I love God, and hateth his brother, he is a liar: for he that*

> *loveth not his brother whom he hath seen, how can he love God whom he hath not seen."*

(I John 4:20)

This passage told me that as a child of God I had to love these two men. I knew with all certainty I was never going to be able to do this in my own power. God revealed the answer to my question of how I was going to love these two men,

> *"For if ye live after the flesh, ye shall die: but if ye through the Spirit do mortify the deeds of the body, ye shall live. For as many as are led by the Spirit of God they are the sons of God."*

(Romans 8:13-14)

Here was my answer. I had to trust the Holy Spirit to take my hate for these two men away. My part was to desire to obey God and love them. Once I did this the Holy Spirit changed the desire in my heart and removed every bit of my hatred for both these men. God used my hatred for these two men to teach me a very valuable lesson. When I truly desire to overcome sin and obey

God, the Holy Spirit will lead me to victory. I now have my reason to love the two men I have spent years hating.

CHAPTER 11 – Learning to Forgive

The next thing God made me aware of was the unforgiveness I had in my heart. Unforgiveness and holding a grudge are pretty much the same thing. The Holy Spirit brought it to my attention that being able to love someone did not always mean I had forgiven them. It is true God loves all of His creation, even the worst unrepentant sinners. Scripture is clear, only God has the position or authority to judge and condemn unrepentant people for their sins. The most quoted verse in the Bible is,

> *"For God so loved the world that He gave His only begotten Son, that whosoever believeth in Him should not perish, but have everlasting life."*

(John 3:16)

My sins were forgiven the moment the Holy Spirit opened my heart to the gospel and I made Jesus the Lord of my life. At that moment in time I was forgiven of every sin I had ever committed or will commit in the future. My pride had blinded me to the commandment in Scripture which tells me I must forgive others just as Jesus forgives me,

> *"For if ye forgive men their trespasses, your heavenly Father will also forgive you: But if ye forgive not men their trespasses, neither will your Father forgive your trespasses."*

(Matthew 6:14-15)

When the Holy Spirit brought this verse to my attention it made me tremble with fear. It says if I fail to forgive others, God will not forgive me. This led me to ask the Holy Spirit to examine my heart and bring every case of unforgiveness to my attention. I must admit I was amazed at what the Holy Spirit revealed to me. There were people whom I truly loved with all my heart that I was harboring unforgiveness against. I was holding things against everyone from my mom to Bubba. I was greatly troubled at how ate up my heart was with the sin of unforgiveness. I have always been kind of a bitter and cranky person, and now I know why.

I knew I had to get all of these grudges out of my heart and find a way to let go of them and forgive every human being who had ever done me wrong. God reminded me it was only through the power of the Holy Spirit I had found a way to love the people I hated most. Now I had to trust Him to show me how to forgive them as well. It is usually easy to say I forgive someone after they tell me they are sorry for what they did. I am finding just because I say "I forgive you" does not always mean I really forgave them. Sometimes I hold on to their transgression, placing it in a special dark place in my heart where it is preserved for revenge at a later date. Thank God the Holy Spirit kicked open the door in my dark room of unforgiveness and shined the light of God on all the grudges I was preserving. I would like to say at that moment everything was changed and all the grudges were removed out of my heart. That was not the case. The light of God showed me how much work I had ahead of me. In my walk with God I have learned forgiving others is an everyday job. Any failure to stay on top of unforgiveness opens the door for bitterness to slowly creep into my heart.

Now when I say I forgive someone for something, I ask the Holy Spirit to make me aware of how my emotions respond when I see the person again.

It still amazes me how many times the first emotion I feel toward those who had wronged me is bitterness which comes from unforgiveness. The thing that shocked me the most was I even had feelings of bitterness toward my friends, as well as my closest family members. The sad thing is they were probably not aware of most of the stuff I was holding against them.

I knew something had to be done about these feelings. I prayed and prayed for God to take them away from me, but they were still there like a cancer eating at my insides. After a while I realized the problem was not that God would not take the unforgiveness from me, the problem was I did not truly want to let it go. My whole life had been spent hating people and keeping an ongoing tally of everything others did to me. I tend to be a little hard headed so it took me a little while to understand the Holy Spirit was telling me I had to re-train my mind and heart. I had to learn a new way of processing other's actions toward me. I must respond the same way God responds when I do something against Him. Just as God forgives me for my sins even when I fail to ask, I have to forgive others even if they do not ask for forgiveness. This can only be done by trusting God, and listening to the Holy Spirit's guidance. The Bible tells me,

> *"I can do all things through Christ which strengtheneth me."*

(Philippians 4:13)

and

> *"Trust in the LORD with all thine heart; and lean not unto thine own understanding. In all thy ways acknowledge Him, and He shall direct thy paths."*

(Proverbs 3:5-6)

At first it was incredibly hard to forgive certain people for things they had done. Now I am learning to cry to God the moment I feel the sin of unforgiveness creeping into my heart. When I see someone who has wronged me I try to be very conscious of how my heart responds to them. If I feel the sin of unforgiveness present I ask God to forgive me. I have to constantly remind myself God has forgiven me for so much, and I have no right to hold anything against anyone else. It does not matter how bad I think what they have done to me is, nothing anyone else has done or will do to me compares to ALL the things I have done to God. Even though I have done all sorts of terrible things to Him, He not only forgives me but has forgotten about my sins and will never hold any of them against me, thanks to the blood of Jesus Christ,

> *"As far as the east is from the west, so far hath He removed our transgressions from us."*

(Psalm 103:12)

God is the only One who has the capability to completely forget the sins committed against Him. In my brain I am unable to forget what others have done to me. It is my heart which must forget the wrongs others have done to me. When my brain sends the message to my heart someone has wronged me, my heart has to send the message back to my brain that I have forgiven them for it. I try my best to make it a habit every time I remember a wrong someone has done to me to remind myself I have forgiven them, and I thank God for forgiving me for my sins. I have to constantly remind myself of how God has forgiven me. Doing this has made it easier to forgive others. The Devil is very crafty. He knows one of my weaknesses is pride and the ability to hold a grudge for a real long time. His attacks on me never stop or seem to lessen, but thanks be to Jesus I am learning to defeat Satan through the power of the Holy Spirit.

After all these years I would like to be able to say forgiving others is easy for me to do, but the truth is I struggle with it every day of my life. Through experience I have learned that when I honestly forgive someone, I get a sense of peace in my heart that words cannot explain. I have found the number one thing that prevents me from forgiving others is pride. The first step I have to take when attempting to overcome the sin of unforgiveness is confessing the sin of pride I have in my heart.

The hardest person I have ever had to try to forgive is myself. God and I are the only two who truly know the depth of the horrible things I have done in my life.

Something I have noticed during my walk with Jesus is Satan does his best to use my past against me in attempts to keep me down.

The Holy Spirit brought it to my attention that if I kept focusing on my past I would never be able to move forward. The Holy Spirit led me to a Scripture that was written by Paul for people like me,

> *"Brethren, I count not myself to have apprehended: but this one thing I do, forgetting those things which are behind, and reaching forth unto those things which are before, I press toward the mark for the prize of the high calling of God in Christ Jesus."*

(Philippians 3:13-14)

God has taught me I cannot live my life looking back on the past. This means I not only can't look back on the way others have wronged me, but I also can't look back on my own mistakes with unforgiveness. I am learning to use my mistakes to propel me forward, not anchor me down. I believe when Jesus tells me,

> *"No man, having put his hands to the*

> *plow, and looking back, is fit for the kingdom of God."*

(Luke 9:62)

He is telling me if I keep looking back where I have stumbled off the row, I will end up completely off course and unusable in the body of Christ. The only way I can live the life Jesus has called me to live, is if I stay completely focused on Him at all times. This is why the Bible makes it clear forgiveness is one of the most important commands a Christian must obey. When I notice the sin of unforgiveness creeping into my heart I remind myself what Jesus says,

> *"If ye forgive not men their trespasses, neither will your Father forgive your trespasses.*

(Matthew 6:15)

CHAPTER 12 – Learning to Tame My Tongue

The Bible makes it abundantly clear, as a Christian I must spend the rest of my life learning to tame my tongue. On the surface this seems like a pretty easy thing to do. I thought it would be easy until I started trying to control the words that came out of my mouth. If cussing were a sport, I would have been a champion. I come from a long line of people who use foul language to express themselves. I learned at a very young age how easy it is to hurt people with my words. My tongue was truly evil and my language incredibly filthy. It is a weapon I was quick to use against others when I was angry, whether friends, foes, or family.

The filth did not just come out when I was angry, my everyday conversations were equally filthy. It was impossible for me to complete a sentence without it including profanity. When I came to prison I found I was not the only one who had received this gift from Satan. Guys in here say some of the most terrible things to one another when playing. It is a game to see who can say the vilest thing to the next guy. As you can imagine what starts off as playing often ends up in a physical altercation. My filthy mouth and I fit right in.

The Holy Spirit used the book of James to bring how I used my tongue to my attention. It is a good idea for every Christian to read the book of James at least once a month. It is there God told me,

> *"If any man among you seem to be religious, and bridleth not his tongue, but deceiveth his own heart, this man's religion is vain."*

(James 1:26)

By claiming to be a Christian I am claiming to be a follower of Jesus Christ, and patterning my life after His. The words that came out of my mouth when I first started my walk were not Christ-like in any way. The Holy Spirit let me know I had to make some serious changes in the way I talked. To be honest I did not think I could ever stop cussing. It seemed like something I had done since I was old enough to talk. Going up against the tongue is full on warfare. It is amazing how many of my emotions seem to be connected to my tongue. The first thing I had to learn to do is separate my emotions from my tongue. I had to pray Job's prayer repeatedly,

> *"Teach me, and I will hold my tongue: and cause me to understand wherein I have erred."*

(Job 6:24)

To be honest I did not think I was ever going to make any advancement on my tongue. It seemed like words just flew out of my mouth before I could stop them. I could be talking in a normal conversation and cuss words would just fall out of my mouth. My problem was I was praying for God to show me the error of my ways, then I was trying to correct them on my own. When it comes to the tongue, James says:

> *"For every kind of beasts, and of birds, and of serpents, and of things in the sea, is tamed, and hath been tamed of mankind: But the tongue can no man tame; it is an unruly evil, full of deadly poison."*

(James 3:7-8)

James says "no man" can tame the tongue. When I first read this verse it made me very frustrated, because if no man could tame the tongue what was I to do about my foul mouth? I took this question to God and He reminded me how I was able to love and forgive others. The only way I could have victory over my tongue is to rely on the Holy Spirit to lead me in my war against my tongue.

I began by asking the Holy Spirit to make me aware every time I cussed. When I was made aware I had cussed I would stop my conversation and ask God to forgive me, every time. Before long it got a little easier not to cuss. I still had a problem when I would get excited while talking to my buddies. I would start cussing seemingly uncontrollably. I knew I needed to pray harder and listen harder for God to give me the answer to how I was to defeat my tongue. I heard the Spirit tell me to pray out loud asking God to forgive me when I cussed, no matter who was around. It was not long until I was able to talk to people without cussing.

I still had a serious problem of controlling my tongue when I got mad at someone. When I would get mad at something or someone filthy hurtful words would fly out of my mouth faster than I could think. Not only would I cuss at them, but I would say very hurtful and cutting things. After one of these encounters I would feel horrible about what I did. Once again I was led to the book of James for help. It is there I am told,

> *"Wherefore, My Beloved brethren, let every man be swift to hear, slow to speak, slow to wrath: For the wrath of man worketh not the righteousness of God."*

(James 1:19-29)

This verse tells me I have to be slow to speak, not only when I am angry but in all situations. I started trying to take three seconds before I would respond to anything, especially when I get mad. This really does work.

When I pause it gives me time to pray and get God involved in the situation. Left on my own I am completely unable to control my mouth, but when I call on God, He is quick to come to my rescue. I used to have a very quick temper. I would fly off the handle over the smallest things. Now that I take a moment before I respond to things I do not get mad nearly as much as I used to. When I do get angry, I get over it a lot quicker now. Not feeding my anger with words seems to starve it and make it go away. I also started making it a habit of telling people I was sorry when I blew up on them. It did not matter if I was in the right or not, I publicly repented of my ungodly actions. This is not a easy thing for me to do. I hate admitting when I am wrong, and I really don't like humbly telling people I am sorry. God has shown me the best way to prevent having to say I'm sorry is to keep my mouth shut.

Since I have started practicing controlling my tongue in the face of confrontation I have learned what the Bible means when it says,

> *"A soft answer turneth away wrath: but grievous words stir up anger."*

(Proverbs 15:1)

People are completely thrown off when I respond to their anger with a soft answer. Not only do I stay calm, but they seem to calm down as well. This is not always easy to do, and I fail often, but I promise you it is a much better way to live rather than responding with hurtful words.

The next part of my tongue the Holy Spirit brought to my attention was my everyday conversations. Although I was not cussing and talking dirty, the conversations I was engaging in were not God edifying on any level. I was and still am amazed at how many conversations I get into that are not fit to have. The Holy Spirit convicted me of my unholy conversations with,

> *"But as He which hath called you is holy, so be ye holy in all manner of conversation; because it is written, Be ye holy; for I am holy."*

(1 Peter 1:15-16)

I ask the Holy Spirit to make me more aware of the conversations I was getting into. I really started paying closer attention to the conversations I was having with people. Thank God I was no longer using filthy language, but the stuff I was talking about was not always God edifying. To be honest the conversations I had with my buddies were very rarely God edifying. I asked the Holy Spirit to bring it to my attention immediately any time the conversations I get into goes to a bad place. I try to step out of the conversations when I catch myself sinning with my tongue. Sometimes this requires getting up and leaving. Gossip, slander, and complaining are the conversations that seem to snare me most often. I have learned a good way to keep out of bad conversations is to avoid hanging out with crowds of people. It is much easier to control or change the conversation when there are only a couple people involved. I also have to avoid letting myself engage in conversations with people who I know like to gossip or complain.

Complaining is very easy to do, especially in prison, and there is always a tasty piece of gossip going around about another inmate or guard. I still struggle with falling into these types of conversations every day of my life. By the grace of God I have learned the only hope I have of controlling my tongue is to keep my mouth shut much more than I talk, and think before I speak. I have found when I filter what I am about to say through the Holy Spirit, I don't have much to say.

CHAPTER 13 – Learning to Trust God

It was not long into my walk with Jesus that I realized the change from the old man to the new man was a lifelong process. It was about two months into my walk when the Holy Spirit first made me understand what Paul means when he says,

> *"And be ye not conformed to this word: but be ye transformed by the renewing of your mind, that ye may prove what is that good, and acceptable, and perfect will of God."*
>
> (Romans 12:2)

Not all of the transformations that had to be made in my life have been battles. Some things I just had to let go of and trust God to take them from me. After I died the thought of ever using heroin never crossed my mind. God completely removed all my desires for that drug. My problem was I still liked to smoke pot. I told myself with all the changes I had been going through I was doing pretty good and deserved to smoke a joint so I could relax from time to time. A few months after I died I had purchased a couple joints. I smoked one of them and got up in my bed to kick back, watch some T.V. and enjoy my high.

God had other plans for me that night. The moment I laid down the Holy Spirit went to work on my heart. He instantly removed all the thoughts of how I deserved to get high. I felt an overwhelming voice telling me that as a child of God I could not partake in any kind of drugs. At that time, me and God had a long conversation about my pot smoking. I tried to explain to Him how I had been given my first taste of pot when I was 10 years old, and I had been smoking it ever since. I told Him how much I loved doing it. Not only did I think I could never give it up, I did not want to give it up. God told me,

> *"Ye cannot drink the cup of the Lord, and the cup of devils: ye cannot be*

partakers of the Lord's table, and of the table of devils. Do we provoke the Lord to jealousy? Are we stronger than He?"

(1 Corinthians 10:21-22)

Deep down I knew I had just lost my argument. My flesh was very stubborn and it was not going down easy. I told God If He wanted me to quit smoking pot He was going to have to take it from me because I was completely unable to do it on my own power. My heavenly Father spoke just two words in my heart "trust me." Very reluctantly I got out of bed and did something I had never done before in my life, I flushed my pot down the toilet, then shut off my T.V. and went to bed pouting.

The next morning I woke up and I knew something had changed inside of me. It did not take me long to figure out what it was. God had completely removed all of my desires to smoke pot. I did not have to fight the urge.

When the guy down the walk offered me a joint, I simply did not want it any more. That was when I realized God was much stronger than my addiction and all I have to do is trust Him with my problem. God made me see my drug use was a form of idol worship. I was relying on dope to do what only God can do. Now when I get all worked up over something I go to my Bible for comfort, and it has always worked for me. Where drugs gave me temporary relief from my troubles, Jesus gives me eternal relief from them.

The next major addiction God took from me was gambling. At this time I was running a poker game, and placing bets on every sport played. This was the way I passed time for many years. One night after a very good night at the poker table, I was kicking back in my bed basking in the glory of how much money I lifted off the other guys that night. All of a sudden the Holy Spirit started talking to me. I tried my hardest to ignore Him, I knew I was not going to like what He was about to tell me. I soon figured out there is no way to ignore God when He wants your attention. Sure enough He got my attention and told me I had to quit all forms of gambling, not just poker.

I spent a good deal of time that night trying to convince God that playing poker was not a bad thing. I played it as a sport just like some people played baseball. God asked me to take a look at the conversations that took place with the people I was spending up to eight hours a day with. He asked me, "Do these conversations bring glory to ME?" He also told me everything about poker was based on deception and,

> *"The wicked worketh a deceitful work: but to him that soweth righteousness shall be a sure reward."*

(Proverbs 11:18)

God made it clear to me that I had been living a wicked and deceitful life on the poker table. He also made it clear that betting on sporting events was not a good way to use the money He had blessed me with. Even after making me aware of all this once again the little boy came out of me and I told God if He wanted me to quit He had to take it. I went to bed that night and had a very peaceful sleep. When I woke up the next morning I did not think about the conversation God and I had the night before. Then when the guys came down and ask if I was ready to get the game started, and before I knew what I was saying I told them I was done playing. Praise be to God the desire to gamble has never returned. Just as He did with my addiction to pot, He cleansed me of every desire I had to gamble.

A few days later as I stood there looking through my collection of CD's trying to figure out what I was going to listen to while I was working out the next day, I heard a familiar voice trying to get my attention. I remember my response as if it happened yesterday, "NOOOO. NOT MY MUSIC!!!" I loved my music and had a pretty impressive collection for prison. As I was in the middle of telling the Holy Spirit all the reasons I was not going to stop listening to my rock and roll music I could sense Him laughing at me. After a few minutes of my whining and a hundred of my excuses, He asked me if the lyrics of the music I spent most of my day listening to brought glory to God in any way? Then He told me I should,

> *"have no fellowship with the unfruitful works of darkness, but rather reprove them."*

(Ephesians 5:11)

At that point I should have said, "Okay, you're right God." But I was still attached to my fleshly desires and not ready to freely give up my music. I told God I would get rid of my music, but I was going to make a list of all my CD's and put a price on them. I told God if I did not get the price I was asking I was not getting rid of them. The next morning I took my list to the recreation yard to try to sell off my CD's. Needless to say the price I had put on them was very high and I did not have any real hope of being able to sell them. I knew a guy who liked that kind of music so I sought him out. When I found him, I showed him the list. He looked and me and said, "Okay." I returned "Okay what?" He said "I will take them all." He did not even haggle over the high price I was asking.

Later that same day, even after seeing God work in my life in such a wonderful way, I put my radio on a station that played rock music. The Holy Spirit filled my heart with such disgust for the words that come out of the musician's mouth I had to change the station. I have never listened to that station again. A short time later I was introduced to a radio station called K LOVE. That was when I learned there is a wide variety of Christian music. Not only is it good for relaxing to, but some of it is excellent for working out to. The best thing about it is, the lyrics are God edifying. Praise be to God, He took all my desires for ungodly music from me and replaced them with music I enjoy listening to more than I ever enjoyed music before.

All three of these events took place within a week's period of time. In these ways God showed me I truly can do all things when I trust Him. I also learned it is possible for God to remove some things out of my life immediately without me having to do anything except give it up to Him. There are some things (fleshly desires) I have to fight every day of my life. I believe God leaves these things in my life to keep me coming to Him every day of my life. God is faithful to never put more on me than I am able to bear when I trust Him. It is through my failures God shows me how much I need Him every moment of my life.

My walk with Jesus has had its ups and downs. There are many things I struggle with, and it seems like I will struggle with them until I am taken home to be with Jesus. I believe God leaves certain struggles in my life to keep me coming to Him and to keep me dependent on Him every day of my life. One thing I have learned in my walk with Jesus is, no matter how many times I fall, His hand is always outstretched to pick me back up again.

God has taught me to never give up, always keep pushing forward. Every moment I live thinking about Jesus is a good moment. Even though I am in prison serving life without parole I am freer now than I have ever been in my life. God has filled all the voids I had in my heart. For the first time in my life I am truly happy and at peace with myself. If you take nothing else from reading this I want you to know it does not matter where you are or what you have done in your life, you will find peace when you dedicate your life to Jesus.

> "Fight the good fight of faith, lay hold on eternal life, whereunto thou art also called, and hast professed a good profession before many witnesses,"
>
> (1 Timothy 6:12)

CHAPTER 14 – Learning to Commit

Before I began my journey with Jesus, the only thing I had ever committed to was doing wrong and getting high. Even when I was a little kid I never committed to anything. For example, I played baseball, and was actually pretty good, but I was never committed to it. Right in the middle of the season my uncle invited me to come down to Oklahoma to stay with him for a few months. I packed my bag and left my team without a second thought.

This became a pattern in my life. I have had jobs that I was good at, and had I stuck with them I could have made a nice living for myself, but I never committed to them. As soon as the job interfered with me wanting to get high or my partying life, I quit. At that time in my life I preferred to be a criminal and do what I pleased, when I pleased. There is not much commitment needed when you are doing wrong. Being a criminal gives you the freedom to walk away from things at a moment's notice. As I said earlier, I even walked away from my own daughter because raising a child interfered with my lifestyle.

My relationships with friends and women were not any different. Usually as soon as things would get a little rocky I would part ways. Before coming to Christ I do not think I ever had a true friend. Sure, I had a lot of so-called 'friends'. It is easy to have friends when you have money to buy the beer, and your bag of weed is always full. I do not think any of the guys in my crowd really cared about each other. Friends don't destroy each other, and that is all me and the crowd I ran with did. We actually looked down on anyone who went to rehab and tried to get their life together. If one of the guys I ran with managed to get clean for a little while, I would actually have feelings of hate toward them.

It is amazing the sense of satisfaction I would get when one of them fell off the wagon and came back to the party. I know that sounds horrible, but it is true. I know

I was not the only one that felt that way because none of my other friends would run that guy off when he came around. No, we just filled up his beer, passed him the joint, or cut an extra long line out for him. Although we called each other friends, we were actually the worst enemies we had.

My relationships with women were not much different. I am ashamed to admit it, but I was never loyal to anyone I was with. I cheated on all the women I was ever with. Some of them I think I loved, or at least cared for, just not enough to solely commit to. I tended to get involved in the most destructive and irrational relationships I could find. It is amazing what kind of effect drug and alcohol use has on a person's mind/life. Looking back I see that none of the behaviors I engaged in were rational at all. But at the time everything I did seemed perfectly rational. The devil is a crafty beast and he knows exactly how to manipulate those who fall into the trap of thinking a little drug or alcohol use is okay. Before long the only thing I was committed to, was feeding the monster inside me.

After I dedicated my life to following Jesus it didn't take me long to realize following Jesus was going to take serious commitment. This created a very serious problem; I knew nothing about true commitment. One day I was reading my Bible and the following verse jumped out at me:

> *"for as ye have yielded your members servants to uncleaness and to iniquity unto iniquity; even so now yield your members servants to righteousness unto holiness."*

(Romans 6:19)

The Holy Spirit used this verse to speak to my heart. At that moment it all made sense to me. The first thirty-four years of my life were spent serving the devil; now the rest of my life is to be spent serving God with total commitment.

At the time I read this verse I was a new Christian and I thought this sounded pretty easy. I did not have any problem serving sin, so I should not have any problem serving God. Right? I mean all I did was switch teams. Right? It did not take long for me to figure out it is a lot easier to be committed to doing wrong than it is to doing right. My struggles at the beginning of my walk were so overwhelming I often wondered if this whole

Christian thing was worth it. Life seemed so much easier when I did not have to pay attention to the words that came out of my mouth, or how I responded to a situation. It was during these times God was most gentle with me and guided my attention back to the love He has shown me. I have learned not to trust in my own ability when it comes to following Jesus.

I have learned to do my best to obey the Psalm that tells me I must:

> *"Commit thy way unto the LORD; Trust also in Him; and He shall bring it to pass."*

(Psalm 37:5)

The Bible has taught me that I am not left to fend for myself on my walk. God is right beside me every step of the way. Over time I have learned God means it when He tells me IF I commit my ways to Him, He will make it happen.

To be honest it took me a while to understand the right interpretation of this passage. For a while I thought it meant "commit 'MY' way to the Lord then 'I' will bring it to pass." This error in thinking led to quite a few spiritual knots on my head. I have learned the first thing I must to do before I commit to something, is take it to the Lord FIRST. I have to make sure it is His will before I take one step. This is done through a lot of praying and Bible reading. The most important lesson I have learned when seeking God's will is to be patient, no matter how long it takes to get my answer. For some reason God does not always answer me as fast as I want Him to. I have learned the biggest part of committing my way to Him is being committed to wait for Him, no matter how long it takes.

When I obey God, commit my way to Him and then wait for His guidance, everything always works out. When I do not commit my way to Him and take off on my own, things never go right. Most of the time when I do not commit my way to God, it is because I already know He is not going to agree with my plans. This is an area in my life I am still working on, and will work on until the day He takes me home.

Over the years God has taught me that no matter how many times I fall down He will always pick me up again and lead me in His way:

"For a just man falleth seven times, and

riseth up again: but the wicked shall fall into mischief."

(Proverbs 24:16)

This verse tells me I will fall, but as a child of the Most High God I will get back up again. The fall is not what I have to focus on. It's the getting back up again I have to concentrate my attention on. Every day I am faced with tough decisions. I have to take all of these decisions to God before I move. More often than not, when I don't take the time to seek God's guidance, I make the wrong decision.

Being a Christian means I also have to pay very close attention to my surroundings. Often I find myself surrounded with guys who are not Christians. The conversations which take place during these times are typically foul and focused on the world. At such times I have to make a choice of whether or not I am going to engage in the conversion, be silent, or move away. I would like to tell you that as a good Christian Soldier I always take off at the first dirty word spoken, but the truth is I don't always leave. Sometimes I even get caught up in the moment and find myself right in the middle of a foul conversation. At that point I have another choice to make. Do I ignore the Spirit and keep right on talking, or do I remove myself from the conversation immediately? It is in that moment I have to choose whether I am going to be committed to the world or to Jesus. Over the years it has gotten easier to flee the conversations. Even more importantly I have found that when I commit my way to the Lord every moment; my way doesn't take me around the places where those conversations are taking place.

Jesus tells me that:

> *"No man having put his hand to the plough, and looking back, is fit for the kingdom of God."*

(Luke 9:62)

The plough is Jesus, and now that I have grabbed a hold of Him I can't look backwards. Jesus wants me to hold on to Him and always keep going forward on a very thin path. Plowing is hard work, and I get tired. Sometimes I trip and fall, but God has taught me to be committed to keeping my hands on the plow and He will drag me along until He reaches down and puts me back on my feet. As long as I keep my hands on the plow I will always be alright, no matter how rough the path gets. Just as a plow opens a furrow in a field for the farmer to plant seed, Jesus opens a furrow in the world for me to plant the seed of the Gospel. Sometimes the soil is soft and it is easy to hang on to the plow, but most of the time the ground is hard, rocky, and uphill. Since I made the commitment to hang on to the plow no matter what, the world has yet to put anything in my path Jesus can't cut through. By trusting in Him I have learned His blade is sharper than anything the world can produce to stop me.

Thanks be to God I now live my life through the power of the Holy Spirit, and I am more committed to God than I ever was to the world. Life is better now than it has ever been, and God had blessed me with a couple of true friends whom I love like brothers.

CHAPTER 15 – Learning to Pray

Ever since I was a very young child I always associated prayer with bad stuff. The only time the word prayer was used around my house was when something bad happened. I remember when I was around twelve years old a very close family friend had a horrible car accident. He was in the hospital and it did not look like he was going to make it. Everyone kept saying we needed to pray for him. I not only had no idea what to pray, I did not know what to expect from my prayers. Eddie passed away from his injuries. At that time I could not help but wonder if he died because I did not pray right.

As I got older my thoughts on prayer continued to be very muddled. Every time I would get in trouble with my parents and later the law, I would pray for God to get me out of it. When I woke up hung over and sick as a dog, I would pray for God to heal me. I cannot count how many times I swore I would not drink again. Of course by noon that same day I would be well. The only thing that left faster than my hangover was my promise to God.

One time some guys tried to rob me and my uncle. This turned into a gun battle. The robbers were outside on the deck shooting into the house, we were inside shooting out. None of us could see what we were shooting at. As I sit and write this, I can still hear the bullets going by my head. I remember praying "God this is real bad. Please help me." Before the prayer was completely finished the bullets stopped. As soon as the bullets stopped I felt like a real gangster, I had just survived my first gun battle. I forgot about God. I did not thank God for getting me out of that jam until a few years ago.

The list of prayers God has answered for me in times of trouble is pretty long. In fact He has probably answered more prayers than I remember praying. The first thirty-four years of my life I had a habit of crying out to Him any time things went really bad. I had trained myself that prayer was for the really bad stuff, everything else I would take care of on my own. I never used prayer as a means to commune with God. Prayer was my ripcord, and when I pulled it I expected God to be my parachute, always saving me right before I crashed to the ground.

My thoughts on prayer completely changed the night I died. Up until that point in my life my prayers were aways from my mind not my heart, and they always concerned my flesh. The night I died my flesh was gone, my cries went out to God from my spirit for the first time in my life. That was when I felt the most empty and alone feeling imaginable. I felt as if God was not there. He had washed His hands of me and I was going to hell. There is no way for me to explain with words the terror my spirit felt that night. All I can tell you is my understanding of prayer completely changed that night. I found out God is not interested in being my parachute, or magic Genie to call on when I need something. God has designed prayer for me to use as a means to communicate with Him in a constant loving Father/son relationship. Even today I still thank God for answering my spirit's prayer that night and bringing me back to life. I know there is no way I can ever repay Him for what He has done for me, but I have vowed to spend the rest of my life living for Him and doing my best to repay Him with my service.

When I started studying the Bible I was amazed at how much it had to say about prayer. It had never occurred to me that even Jesus prayed to the Father:

> *"and in the morning, rising up a great while before day, He went out, and departed into a solitary place, and there prayed."*
>
> (Mark 1:35)

Everything Jesus did was done as an example for what I am to do. So now I get up an hour earlier and spend some time in prayer every day. I have found the morning is the best time for quiet prayer. It is good for me to get with God before all of the events of the day start weighing on my thoughts. Also, I am more receptive to His voice at that time. One of the most valuable lessons I have learned is, prayer is not just about me talking to God, it is also a time for me to listen to God talk to me.

Another of the awesome lessons I have learned over the years is prayer is not for just when I am in trouble. Prayer is something I can do all day, every day. I have learned not to make one decision until I take it to God in prayer. I try to imagine prayer as the fuel that keeps my spiritual motor running. Prayer starts it first thing in the morning and then constant prayer keep it running all day and night. Prayer is what fuels my spiritual relationship with God. David tells us in the Psalms:

> *"As for me, I will call upon God; and the LORD shall save me. Evening, and morning and at noon, will I pray, and cry aloud: and He shall hear my voice."*

(Psalm 55:16-17)

The most satisfying thought a person can have is to know God hears His children anytime we call out to Him. Throughout Scripture we are told to "walk in the Spirit." I never understood what that meant until I learned what the true purpose for prayer is. Prayer is the method God has appointed for me to use to be in constant communion with Him. Walking in the Spirit means to be walking in prayer. The only way I can walk in the Spirit is to be open to the Spirit's guidance. Now that I am saved by grace through faith in Jesus Christ, I have access to God 24 hours a day, 7 days a week. The Bible says:

> *"Therefore being justified by faith, we have peace with God through our Lord Jesus Christ: By whom also we have access by faith into this grace wherein we stand, and rejoice in hope of the glory of God."*

(Romans 5:1-2)

AND

> *"Let us therefore come boldly unto the throne of grace that we may obtain mercy, and find grace to help in time of need."*

(Hebrews 4:16)

Being saved does not just mean I am going to heaven. It means I now have open access to God all day, every day. Nothing I face in my day is too big or too small to take to God. I get great comfort when I talk to God about the things that are going on in my day. I tell Him when I am stressed out, angry, sad, lonely, hurt, happy, or thankful for an answered prayer. I talk to Him when I am at a crossroads and must decide which way to turn.

It is comforting for me to know Jesus felt every emotion I feel, plus some. Jesus even knows what it is like to have the Father tell Him no. The night Jesus was betrayed and about to be tortured and murdered on the cross He asked His father if there was any way He could avoid what was about to happen:

> *"He went away again the second time, and prayed, saying, O my father, if this cup may not pass away from Me, except I drink it, thy will be done."*
>
> (Matthew 26:42)

God told Jesus no, there was no other way for mankind to be saved. He had to stay on earth and allow Himself to be tortured and killed. Jesus did not cry and complain. He did not call down legions of angels to rescue Him. He willingly submitted to the Father's will. This is what I have to do when God tells me no. Believe me God tells me no quite a bit. Anytime my prayers are not in line with His will, He tells me no.

Over time I have learned to filter my desires through prayer. When I pray I ask myself two questions: First, what would Jesus do; and second, am I wanting to satisfy my flesh, or please God? I have found that most of the time God tells me no, it's because my prayer is flesh driven and Scripture says:

> *"Ye ask, and receive not, because ye ask amiss, that ye may consume it upon your lusts."*
>
> (James 4:3)

The only time God answers my prayers and gives me what I want is when my prayers are in accordance with His will.

Another thing I have learned about praying is that I do not have to get all fancy and try to impress God with long-winded prayers. God knows me better than anyone, and He certainly knows how I talk. God does not want me to become someone else when I pray. He wants me to be myself when I talk to Him. If my daily speech is not worthy to take before God then I need to change my speech. It is pleasurable to talk to God as my loving Father. Looking back I imagine God got a real good belly laugh at some of my prayers when I first started learning to pray. For a good understanding on how to pray and how to listen to God through prayer, I highly recommend Charles Stanley's book *"Learning to Listen to God."* Reading this book changed my prayer life. My relationship with God has greatly improved since learning to pray and listen to God better. The only way I am able to get through everyday walking with Jesus is by obeying His command to:

"PRAY WITHOUT CEASING"

(1 Thessalonians 5:17)

CHAPTER 16 – Learning Who Jesus Is

Very early in my walk with Jesus a guy that is of another faith approached me and asked if I was interested in buying some dope. I told him "No. That is not part of my life any more. I am a Christian now." My response started a conversation with him about God. I was holding my own pretty good until he asked me who I thought Jesus was. I told him Jesus is God. He told me I was a fool for believing something like that. He tried to convince me Jesus was a good man who lived a holy life, and served the role of a prophet sent from God, but He was not God. Sadly I was completely unable to defend my position that Jesus is God.

I remembered being told Jesus is God when I went to Sunday school as a little boy. Preachers say it all the time and I had read it in many books. In my heart I know Jesus is God, but I cannot defend the point based on what someone else told me, or what I feel. As a Christian I have to be able to defend the fact Jesus is God from the Scriptures. So I started searching the Bible to see what it says on the subject of Jesus being God. The first question I had to answer was: is Jesus Omnipotent [almighty/all powerful]?

When Jesus and His disciples were crossing the sea, a storm came upon them that was rocking the ship to the point the disciples thought they were about to sink. This had to be a pretty bad storm for John, Peter and Andrew to have been worried. These men were seasoned fishermen and had spent their lives on the water. In a panic they went searching for Jesus. I can imagine their surprise when they found Him sleeping peacefully in the stern of the ship. I wonder if there was any debate about who was going to wake Him up and tell him they were scared. We are told in the Bible that:

> *"His disciples came to Him and awoke Him, saying, Lord, save us: we perish. And He saith unto them, Why are ye fearful, O ye of little faith? Then He arose, and rebuked the winds and the*

> *sea; and there was a great calm."*

(Matthew 8:25-26)

Jesus rebuked the weather and sea like a parent rebukes a child. When He said "cut it out" the weather and sea immediately obeyed Him. This shows that Jesus is in control of the weather and the seas. Throughout Scripture the only one that has power over the weather and the sea is God. In (Exodus 14:21-28) God parted the sea for the Jews when they were fleeing Egypt.

The Bible is clear: Jesus has power over the weather and seas as only God does.

The next thing I found was Jesus' power over sickness. The Bible says:

> *"Now when the sun was setting, all they that had any sick with diver's diseases brought them unto Him; and He laid His hands on every one of them, and healed them."*

(Luke 4:40)

The Bible does not say Jesus healed "some of them," it

says He healed every one of them. This verse is not the only one in the Bible that tells of Jesus healing people. The first thing He did when entering a town was heal all of their sick. When I started studying the manner in which Jesus healed the sick, blind, lepers, and cripples I was amazed at the completeness of the healings. For example:

> *"And a certain man was there, which had an infirmity thirty and eight years. When Jesus saw him lie, and knew that he had been now a long time in that case, He saith unto him, Wilt thou be made whole? The impotent man answered Him, Sir, I have no man, when the water is troubled, to put me into the pool: but while I am coming, another steppeth down before me. Jesus saith unto him, Rise, take up thy bed and walk. And immediately the man was made whole, and took up his bed, and walked."*

(John 5:5-9)

This man had been lying on a bed for 38 years. By that

time all his leg muscles would have been gone. He would not have known how to walk even if he could stand up. Jesus not only healed him, He put muscles in the man's legs and gave his brain the knowledge of how to walk instantly. Anyone who has ever suffered an injury that required rehab knows how miraculous this healing was.

Jesus also had power over all devils and evil spirits:

> *"And devils also came out of many, crying out, and saying, Thou art Christ the Son of God, And He rebuking them suffered them not to speak: for they knew that He was Christ."*

(Luke 4:41)

Jesus also had the power and authority to give his disciples power over all manner of sickness and evil spirits:

> *"Then He called His twelve disciples together, and gave them power and authority over all devils, and to cure diseases."*

(Luke 9:1)

> *"And the seventy returned again with Joy, saying, Lord, even the devils are subject into us THROUGH THY NAME."*

(Luke 10:17)

Jesus raised the dead three times (Luke 7:14-15; John 11:43-44; Matthew 9:18-26). These passages show that Jesus has power over life and death.

The works Jesus did in the presence of numerous witnesses prove beyond any doubt that Jesus is Omnipotent.

Next I turned my attention to see what the Bible says about who Jesus is. One of the most convincing passages in the Bible regarding who Jesus is, is:

> *"in the beginning was the Word, and the Word was with God, and the Word was God."*

(John 1:1)

AND

> *"And the Word was made flesh, and dwelt among us, (and we beheld His glory. The glory as of the only begotten of the Father,) Full of grace and truth."*

(John 1:14)

Scripture is clear that Jesus is "The Word" and John is clear that "The Word is God come in flesh." Thomas, who is known as the most skeptical of all the disciples, made one of the greatest statements ever uttered by man. At first he did not believe the disciples when they told him Jesus was risen. He told them unless he shoved his hand into Jesus' side he would not believe He was risen. Imagine his surprise when Jesus stood before him and said:

> *"Reach hither thy finger, and behold my hands; and reach hither thy hand, and thrust it into my side: and be not faithless, but believing. And Thomas answered and said unto Him, MY LORD AND MY GOD."*

(John 20:27-28)

Thomas does not call Jesus his 'prophet' or his 'good

teacher' or any of the other false titles man has attempted to give Jesus. Thomas called Jesus his "Lord" and "his God." This is not the only time Jesus was worshipped as God. (SEE Matthew 14:33; Matthew 28:9; Hebrews 1:6; Revelation 5:12-14). These verses show that man, angels, and every being in heaven worships Jesus. The Scriptures are clear that there is only one God who is to be worshipped:

> *"Thou shalt have no other gods before Me. Thou shalt not make unto thee any graven image, or any likeness of anything that is in heaven above, or that is in the earth beneath, or that is In the water under the earth: Thou shalt not bow down thyself to them, nor serve them: for I the LORD thy God am a jealous God."*

(Exodus 20:3-5)

Jesus never corrected anyone for bowing down and worshipping Him. Thus He was worshipped as God by man.

Next I looked at the statements Jesus made in regards to

Himself. He made many statements as to who He is in relation to the Father:

> *"I and My Father are one."*
>
> (John 10:30)
>
> *"if ye had known Me, ye should have known my Father also."*
>
> (John 8:19)
>
> *"And he that seeth Me seeth Him that sent Me."*
>
> (John 12:45)
>
> *"He that hateth Me hatheth My Father also."*
>
> (John 15:23)

The next fact that got my attention is that Jesus had the authority to forgive sins. Which is something only God can do:

> *"When Jesus saw their faith, He said unto the sick of the palsy, Son, thy sins be forgiven thee."*
>
> (Mark 2:5)

AND

> *"And He said unto her, Thy sins are forgiven."*

(Luke 7:48)

I believe the Scriptures make it clear Jesus was, is and always will be God. The night in the manger when Jesus was born, God came into the world as a baby. That baby grew into a man, and that man was fully God. The fact that Jesus is God made in the flesh makes Him alone able to be the perfect sacrifice to cover the sins of all who call upon His name. Now He is raisen from the dead and sits at the right hand of the Father. The Bible reveals God in three persons:

> *"And there are three that bear record in heaven, the Father, the Word, and the Holy Ghost: AND THESE THREE ARE ONE."*

(1 John 5:7)

Exactly how God is three Persons in One is beyond my understanding. A lot of the things God has done and will do are beyond my understanding. One of the most important lessons God has taught me in my walk with

Him is that just because I do not understand something does not mean I can ignore it or deny it: My job is to trust God and believe what He says. The Bible is very clear Jesus is God made flesh and is,

"the image of the invisible God,"

(Colossians 1:15)

CHAPTER 17 – Learning Why I should Trust the Bible

Ever since I was little, going to church with my grandparents, I always believed the Bible was right. I think part of the reason I believed was because everyone in the church said it was right. To be honest I never really gave it much thought until about a year into my walk with Jesus.

I was engaged in a conversation with a guy who claimed to believe in all religions. He believed all paths led to heaven. As long as a person was true to what they believed they would go to heaven. I asked him what he thought about the verse in the Bible where Jesus says:

"I am the way, the truth, and the life: no

> *man cometh unto the Father, but by me."*

(John 14:6)

His response was that the Bible was a good book, but it was created by men to control others. He believed the Bible was a tool used by the government to control the masses. As incorrect as his statement was, I was unable to defend my position that the Bible is the Word of God. I knew it and believed it with all my heart, I just could not defend it. So I set out to educate myself so I could defend why I believe the Bible is the Word of God.

I started from the outside looking in and found that the Bible is composed of 66 books. The Old Testament has 39 books, with 927 chapters, that have been broken down into 23,214 verses. It was written between 1400 B.C. and 400 B.C. The New Testament has 27 books, with 260 chapters, that have been broken down into 7,959 verses. It was written between 50 A.D. and 100 A.D. The books in the Bible were written by over 40 different men. These men lived on three different continents (Asia, Europe, and Africa). The Bible was written over a 1,400 year period. Many of the men who wrote the books in the Bible never had any contact with one another. As I said, some of them lived on different continents. They did not have phones back then. The Bible was written in three different languages. The Old Testament was written in Hebrews with two passages in Daniel written in Aramaic. The New Testament was written in Greek.

Even though these men were separated by many years, cultures, and languages, they all had the same message. The Bible is one Book, teaching one plan of grace. All the writers of the Old Testament point to salvation for mankind through the coming of Jesus. All the writers of the New Testament tell of the life of Jesus and how the only way to be saved is through faith in Him. Both the Old and New Testaments instruct mankind on how to live life pleasing to God. John MacArthur breaks down the five recurring motifs that are constantly emphasized throughout the Bible as: the character of God; the judgment for sin and disobedience; the blessing for faith and obedience; the Lord Savior and sacrifice for sin; the coming kingdom and glory. Everything written in the Bible points to one or more of these five points. All the writers of the Bible were in agreement on all five of these points. The Bible never contradicts itself.

The Old Testament contains approximately 330 references to Jesus that are cited in the New Testament either as predictions fulfilled in Jesus' life and ministry or as previsions of His character. The Wycliffe Bible Dictionary says, "According to the law of mathematical probability there would be one chance in
84,000,000,000,000,000,000,000,000,000,000,000,000,
000,000,000,000,000,000,000,000,000,000,000,000,000
,000,000,000,000,000,000,000 that all these predictions would occur in the case of a single individual."

The following is a list of over a hundred Old Testament prophecies of the Messiah that were fulfilled by Jesus. (Source: "The Strongest Strong's Concordance")

I would strongly suggest a person take the time to sit down and look up at least some of these prophecies. As I read through them I quickly noticed the perfect accuracy with which Jesus fulfilled them. The prophecies in the Bible are not vague. They are very specific, and Jesus fulfilled them with the perfection only God could, time and time again.

PROPHECIES	FULFILLED IN
Genesis3:15	Luke 22:53
Genesis3:15	Hebrews 2:14;
1 John 3:8	Genesis12:3
Acts 3:25	Galatians 3:8
Genesis13:15	Galatians 3:15-19
Genesis14:18-20	Hebrews 7
Genesis18:18	Acts 3:25
Galatians 3:8	Genesis22:18
Acts 3:25	Galatians 3:8
Genesis49:10	Luke 1:32-33
Exodus12:1-14,46	John 19:31-36; 1 Corinthians5:7; 1 Peter1:19; Exodus16:4; John 6:31-33
Exodus24:8	Hebrews 9:11-29
Leviticus15:15-17	Romans3:25; Hebrews 9:1-14, 24 1 John 2:2
Numbers 21:8-9	John 3:14-15

Numbers 24:17	Luke 1:32-33
Numbers 24:17	Revelation22:16
Deuteronomy 18:17	John 6:14; 12:49-50; Acts 3:22-23
Deuteronomy 21:23	Galatians 3:13
Deuteronomy 30:12-14	Romans10:6-8
Samuel 7:14	Hebrews 1:5
Samuel 7:16	Luke 1:32-33; Revelation 19:11-16
1 Chronicles17:13	Hebrews 1:5
1 Chronicles17:14	Luke 1:32-33; Revelation 19:11-16
Psalm 2:7	Matthew 3:17; 17:5; Mark 1:11; 9:7;
	Luke 3:22; 9:35; Acts 13:33;
	Hebrews 1:5
Psalm 2:9	Revelation 2:27
Psalm 8:2	Matthew 21:16
Psalm 8:4-5	Hebrews 2:6-9
Psalm 8:6	Corinthians 15:27-28
	Ephesians1:22

Psalm 16:8-11	Acts 2:25-32; 13:35-37
Psalm 22:1	Matthew 27:46; Mark 15:34
Psalm 22:7-8	Matthew 27:29; 27:41-44;
	Mark 15:18; 15:29-32;
	Luke 23:35-39
Psalm 22:18	Matthew 27:35; Mark 15:34;
	Luke 23:34; John 19:24
Psalm 22:22	Hebrews 2:12
Psalm 31:5	Luke 23:46
Psalm 34:20	John 19:31-36
Psalm 35:19	John 15:25
Psalm 40:6-8	John 6:38; Hebrews 10:5-9
Psalm 41:9	John 13:18
Psalm 45:6-7	Hebrews 1:8-9
Psalm 68:18	Ephesians 4:7-11
Psalm 69:4	John 15:25
Psalm 69:9	John 2:14-22

Psalm 69:21	John 19:29
Psalm 69:25	Acts 1:20
Psalm 78:2	Matthew 13:34-35
Psalm 102:25-27	Hebrews 1:10-12
Psalm 110:1	Acts 2:34-35; 1 Corinthians 15:25; Ephesians 1:20-22; Hebrews 1:13; 10:12-13
Psalm 110:1	Matthew 22:41-45; Mark 12:35-37; Luke 20:41-44
Psalm 110:4	Hebrews 5:6; 7:11-22
Psalm 118:22-23	Matthew 21:42-44; Mark 12:10; Luke 20:17-19; Acts 4:10-11; 1 Peter2:7-8
Psalm118:26	Matthew 21:9; Mark 11:9; Luke 19:38; John 12:13
Isaiah 6:9-10	Matthew 13:14-15; Mark 4:12; Luke 8:10; John 12:37-41

Isaiah 7:14	Matthew 1:18; Luke 1:26-35
Isaiah 8:14	Romans 9:32-33; 1 Peter2:7-8
Isaiah 9:1-2	Matthew 4:13-16; Mark 1:14-15; Luke 4:14-15
Isaiah 9:6-7	Luke 1:32-33
Isaiah 9:7	John 1:1,18
Isaiah 9:7	Ephesians 2:14-17
Isaiah 11:1-2	Matthew 3:16; Mark 1:16; Luke 3:21-22
Isaiah 11:10	Luke 1:32-33
Isaiah 11:10	Romans 15:12
Isaiah 22:22	Revelation 3:7
Isaiah 25:8	1 Corinthians 15:54
Isaiah 28:16	Romans 9:32-33; 1 Peter2:6
Isaiah 35:5-6	Matthew 11:4-6, Luke 7:22
Isaiah 40:3-5	Matthew 3:3; Mark 1:3; Luke 3:4; John 1:23

Isaiah 42:1-4	Matthew 12:15:21
Isaiah 45:23	Romans 14:11; Philippians 2:10
Isaiah 49:6	Acts 13:46—47
Isaiah 50:6	Matthew 27:26-30; Mark 14:65; 15:15,19; Luke 22:63; John 19:1-3
Isaiah 50:6	Matthew 26:67; Mark 14:65
Isaiah 53:1	John 12:38; Romans 10:16
Isaiah 53:3	John 1:11
Isaiah 53:4-5	Matthew 8:16-17; Mark 1:32-34; Luke 4:40-41; 1 Peter 2:24
Isaiah 53:7-8	John 1:29,36; Acts 8:30-35; 1 Peter 1:19; Revelation 5:6,12
Isaiah 53:9	Hebrews 4:15; 1 Peter 2:22
Isaiah 53:9	Matthew 27:57-60
Isaiah 53:12	Matthew 27:38; Mark 15:27-28; Luke 22:37; 23:33; John 19:18
Isaiah 55:3	Luke 22:20; 1 Corinthians 11:25

Isaiah 55:3	Acts 13:33
Isaiah 59:20-21	Romans 11:26-27
Isaiah 60:1-3	Matthew 2:11; Romans 15:8-12
Isaiah 61:1-2	Matthew 4:16; Mark 1:10; Luke 4:18-21
Isaiah 65:1	Romans 10:20
Isaiah 65:2	Romans 10:21
Jeremiah 23:5	Luke 1:32-33
Jeremiah 23:6	Matthew 1:21
Jeremiah 23:6	1 Corinthians 1:30
Jeremiah 31:15	Matthew 2:16-18
Jeremiah 31:31-34	Luke 22:20; 1 Corinthians 11:25; Hebrews 8:8-12; 10:15-18
Jeremiah 32:40	Luke 22:20; 1 Corinthians 11:25
Jeremiah 33:15	Luke 1:32-33
Jeremiah 33:16	Matthew 1:21
Jeremiah 33:16	1 Corinthians 1:30

Ezra 21:26-27	Luke 1:32:33
Ezra 34:23-24	John 10:11,14,16; Hebrews 13:20
	1 Peter 5:4
Ezra 37:24-25	John 10:11,14,16; Hebrews 13:20;
	1 Peter 5:4
Ezra 37:26	Luke 22:20; 1 Corinthians 11:25
Daniel 7:13-14	Matthew 24:30; 26:64; Mark 13:26;14:62;
	Luke 21:27; Revelation 1:13; 14:14
Daniel 7:27	Revelation 11:15
Daniel 9:24-26	Galatians 4:4
Hosea 11:1	Matthew 2:14-15
Joel 2:28-32	Acts 2:14-21
Amos 9:11-12	Acts 15:13-18
John 1:17	Matthew 12:39-40
Micah 5:2	Matthew 2:1-6
Micah 5:2	Luke 1:32-33
Micah 5:4	John 10:11,14

Micah 5:5	Ephesians 2:14-17
Zechariah 9:9	Matthew 21:1-9; Mark 11:1-10; Luke 19:28-38; John 12:12-16
Zechariah 11:12-13	Matthew 27:1-10
Zechariah 12:10	John 19:37; Revelation1:7
Zechariah 13:7	Matthew 26:31; 26:55-56; Mark 14:27; 14:48-50
Malachi 3:1	Matthew 11:7-10; Mark 1:2-4; Luke 7:24-27
Malachi 4:5-6	Matthew 11:14; 17:11-13; Mark 9:11-13; Luke 1:16-17

The next question I set out to answer was: How were the sixty-six books of the Bible put together. The books of the Old Testament were compiled by the time Jesus came into the world. Jewish tradition holds that Ezra compiled the books of the Old Testament in approximately 457-444 B.C.

The books of the New Testament were compiled at the council of Laodicea in 363 A.D., and in 387 A.D. at the council of Carthage. These councils were made up of the most learned scholars and church leaders of that time. They used a four part test when establishing whether a book was to be accepted as the Word of God.

1. Authors who were in direct contact with Jesus or the Apostles.
2. Consistency in doctrine, and evidence of being inspired by the Holy Spirit.
3. Wide acceptance and use by churches in all regions, under the guidance of the Holy Spirit.
4. It must have produced dynamic changes in the lives of people, as used by the Holy Spirit.

When these councils met they spent a lot of time in prayer and fasting.

They placed all of their trust in the Holy Spirit to guide them. I believe the fact their work has survived almost 2,000 years, and has led more people to saving faith than any other writings, is all the evidence needed to prove that they were acting under the guidance of the Holy Spirit. The Bible is the Word of God given to mankind. The Bible is not the work of man:

"All Scripture is given by inspiration of

> *God, and is profitable for doctrine, for reproof, for correction, for instruction in righteousness: That the man of God may be perfect, thoroughly furnished unto all good works."*

(2 Timothy 3:16-17)

This passage tells me that every single word that is written in the Bible is designed to guide me into being the person God created me to be. The Bible is not just another book. It was crafted by God to stand forever:

> *"For all flesh is as grass, and all the glory of man as the flower of grass. The grass withereth, and the flower thereof falleth away: But the Word of the Lord endureth for ever, And this is the Word which by the gospel is preached unto you."*

(1 Peter 1:24-25)

It was only after I began to truly understand that the Bible is the true perfect Word of God that it has had its biggest impact on my life. Whereas I use to dread reading the Bible, now I look forward to my time in the

Scriptures every day. Most generally when I pray I do all the talking to God, but when I read the Bible, that is when God talks to me. Since I have started having a regular Bible reading time every day, my relationship with God has grown beyond anything I ever imagined it would be. I now have an understanding of what God's will is. When I am in doubt about something going on in my life I can always find my answer in the pages of the Bible. I have learned to lean on and trust God's Word with all my heart. It has never led me wrong, and I know it never will.

> *"Thy Word is very pure: therefore thy servant loveth it."*

(Psalm 119:140)

CLOSING THOUGHTS

My reason for writing this was to show God's forgiveness knows no boundaries. I was a foul talking, thieving, robbing, murderer, and God shined His grace into my heart through the Blood of Jesus Christ. None of us are worthy of salvation. It does not matter how "good" we live. The only way to be saved is to call on the name of Jesus, and not only call on Him, but make Him the Lord of our life.

It does not matter what sins you have committed in your life, or what sins you are currently trapped in, God will not only forgive you, He will help you to overcome your addictions. All you have to do is call on Him with a cry from your heart. If you are tired of being a slave to the devil and the cares of the world, call on Jesus and become a servant of the Most High God.

The time for your salvation is RIGHT NOW THIS SECOND. Tomorrow might be too late. God blessed me with the second chance to get it right. Not many people get a second chance to obtain eternal life with Jesus. For most, once we take our last breath it's all over, we are either going to hell to suffer for all eternity, or we are going to heaven to spend eternity living in peace and joy in the presence of Jesus. The human mind cannot comprehend the glory that we will experience in heaven. Right now is the time to examine your heart and see if you are saved. Look at your life and measure it against the Word of God. The Bible makes it clear what the life of a Christian looks like. The Bible is the only thing we are to rest our salvation on. It does not matter how much better or worse we are than our neighbor. The only thing that will matter in the end is, whether you have been washed in the blood of Jesus.

If you are not sure where you stand I would strongly suggest you get down on your knees right now, wherever you are, and pray; "Father, I am a lost sinner. I am completely helpless to save myself. Through the power of the Holy Spirit I call on the name of Jesus to please save me from my sins. Father, please save me and seal me with Your Holy Spirit. Father open the eyes and ears of my heart so I can hear your Spirit as it guides me through life. Thank you for your mercy."

If you have just prayed this prayer there are three things you need to do. First thing is to get a Bible and start getting to know the God you now serve. I would suggest starting in the New Testament at the book of John. The next thing you need to do is get involved with a local church. It is very important to get in a Bible preaching church. Two things you are responsible for when choosing a church is, listening to the Holy Spirit in your heart, and testing what the preacher says to the Bible. This requires Bible study on your part. It is unwise for a Christian to believe everything someone tells them about the Bible. The third thing you need to do is pray all the time. Learn to talk to God before you make any decisions. You are now a child of the Most High God, and He will be right there with you every moment of your life. All you have to do is pray, then listen. I pray that God will bless you and guide your every step. I look forward to seeing you in heaven.

With all my love,

Your Brother in Jesus Christ,
Barry J. Holcomb/Christian Mann

BARRY J. HOLCOMB'S OTHER WRITINGS

Barry Holcomb has also authored a verse by verse commentary of the New Testament. His commentary is the final product of a four year labor of love. It was written to help both new believers as well as seasoned Bible readers a deeper understanding of the Bible. The commentary is titled "Exploring God's Word: A New Testament Commentary." It is available at Midnight Express Books, or at Amazon.com.

Barry Holcomb also writes a monthly news letter titled, "Dear Neighbor." It can be viewed on Facebook at Christian Mann. If you have any questions or comments you can contact Barry directly at:

Barry J. Holcomb 514068

South Central Correction Center

255 West Highway 32

Licking, Missouri 65542

To order additional copies of this book or Barry's 1st book,
please send check or money order to:

Midnight Express Books
POBox 69
Berryville AR 72616

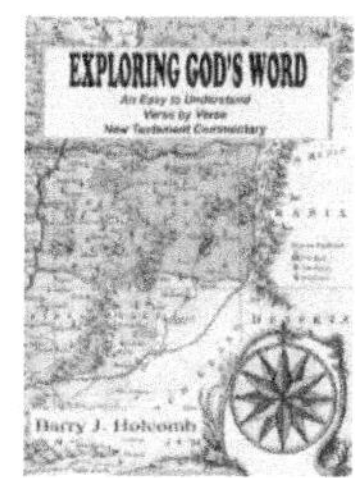

QTY ORDERED

_____ Exploring God's Word $14.95 $__________

_____ Thought I was A Christian
But I went to Hell $10.95 $__________

Subtotal $__________

How many books are you ordering?
_______ x $3.99 = $__________

MEB processing fee
How many books are you ordering?
_______ x $1.50 = $__________

TOTAL ENCLOSED $__________

Ship to:
NAME ______________________________
ADDRESS ______________________________
____

Made in the USA
Monee, IL
19 September 2021

77633348R20115